How to Be an Imperfectionist

The New Way to Self-Acceptance, Fearless Living, and Freedom from Perfectionism

By Stephen Guise

Blog
http://deepexistence.com

Book site
http://imperfectionistbook.com

Copyright

How to Be an Imperfectionist by Stephen Guise

Legal Disclaimer

More from Stephen

Get My Stress Management eBook for Free
In addition to receiving *Stress Management Redefined* and other gifts instantly, every Tuesday, subscribers get an email containing smart life strategies (which go beyond motivation). People have told me the content is life-changing, and it's free! The benefit for me is communication: I'll have a way to tell you when my next book or course is available.

Sign up here: **http://deepexistence.com/subscribe/**

Mini Habits
If you haven't yet, I strongly recommend reading my first book, *Mini Habits*. While it's not imperative to read *Mini Habits* to benefit from this book, there is a definite synergy between them. If you read *Mini Habits*, you'll understand why these imperfectionist solutions are in mini habit form.

Based on the science, *Mini Habits* is arguably the most effective habit formation strategy in the world; and based on reviews, it's arguably the most beloved. People can't help but talk about the strategy that's changed their life!

Mini Habits Book: **http://amazon.com/dp/B00HGKNBDK**

Mini Habit Mastery
If you prefer video and want to learn the mini habits concept, you can take the Mini Habit Mastery Video Course. It retails for $149, but you can use coupon code **"imperfectionist"** to get it for just $59 (that's $90 off!). The book and the course are leaders in ratings and satisfaction (the course is rated 5 stars from 40+ reviews), and I guarantee my products' reviews are genuine.

Mini Habit Mastery HD Video Course: **http://udemy.com/mini-habit-mastery/**

Table of Contents

Preface

"Strive for continuous improvement, instead of perfection."

~ Kim Collins

Perfectionism (noun): "A disposition to regard anything short of perfection as unacceptable"[1]

Having perfectionistic tendencies myself, I know how destructive and frustrating this mindset can be. In this book, I want to make a case that not only compels you but also shows you how to embrace imperfection in your life. Imperfection isn't bad, it's freedom. (To be clear, "perfection" isn't bad either—by definition, it's flawless—but perfectionism is problematic.)

Perfectionism makes you stay home, not take chances, and procrastinate on projects; it makes you think your life is worse than it is; it keeps you from being yourself; it stresses you out; it tells you that good is bad; and it ignores the natural way in which things work.

We're going to discuss strategies that can help us to become imperfectionists. Before we get into this book, there are some things about my first book that will be relevant to our journey into imperfectionism.

The Power of Mini Habits

Mini Habits: Smaller Habits, Bigger Results is about a strategy for lasting habitual change. As a result of the strategy's effectiveness, *Mini Habits* has been a great success both commercially and in the lives of the people who implement the strategy. After selling more than 45,000 copies in its first year in the United States, it is being translated into more than a dozen languages worldwide.

The premise of *Mini Habits* was ridiculous: force yourself to do (seemingly) too-small-to-matter positive behaviors, but ones you can do every day, even on your worst day. Keep this in mind as I refer to mini habits throughout this book: a mini habit is a too-small-to-fail behavior you do every day.

Daily mini habit examples: write one line of code, read two pages in a book, write 50 words, call one lead (sales), email one person (networking), or process one piece of mail. The list goes on at minihabits.com/mini-habit-ideas, but the concept is the same—choose an activity you can't possibly fail to do, and do it until it becomes a habit and grows into something bigger. There is no ceiling on mini habits, as your one push-up goal can turn into 50 push-ups on any given day. The small goal only ensures that you start.

My Exciting Results with Mini Habits
As I write this more than two years after doing that first single push-up, I want to share how my results have continued to get *better* over time with mini habits.

After six months of doing one push-up (or more) per day, my resistance to exercising had decreased. I was then able to go to the gym three days a week; three months later, I went to the gym four days a week; two months after that, I was going five days a week. At first, these were requirements I needed to meet. I still exercise three to five days a week because I want to do it, and it's often for an hour or more. Exercise is like eating dinner: I may end up skipping it once in a while for unforeseen reasons, such as illness or injury, but if I can do it, I won't skip it. I'm in the best shape of my life, and I'm getting stronger.

On the heels of my exercising mini habit's success, I began mini habits of reading two pages of a book and writing 50 words a day. More than a year later, I haven't raised the targets on these because it isn't necessary. I still read and write every day. The amount varies, but the results have been consistently greater than expected, which I've seen is common with mini habits. Small, consistent, incremental steps in a healthy direction bring big results.

There's been an exciting spillover effect into my psyche. I have more confidence in social situations, both from the above life improvements and by learning to take small steps to move ahead in any situation that scares me. Even as a natural-born introvert who is capable of hibernating for long periods, and someone who does not excel at small talk (I'm an INTP for those familiar with Myers-Briggs personality profiling), I've gone from shy to social.

My comfort zone is constantly expanding in multiple areas. I'm more comfortable with (and more willing to do) what matters most to me: exercising, eating healthy food, writing, reading, and socializing. Before and after photos are great at capturing weight loss, but no photo can capture the many internal shifts that take place when you practice mini habits for a year or two. And unlike 21- or 30-day programs, these are permanent lifestyle changes. This has all happened over a period of two years without a slip-up.

I've made more personal progress in the last couple of years than in the 10 before them. It's because mini habits work on so many levels to move life forward, and they rarely fail those who try them out.

This book has numerous ties to *Mini Habits*, but the focus is not directly on forming habits. The focus of *How to Be an Imperfectionist* is on specific solutions to the widespread problem of perfectionism.

From Mini Habits to Imperfectionism

Here's a specific example of how mini habits have made me more of an imperfectionist: I was headed to the grocery store one day, and my gym was next door to it. I wanted to exercise that day, but I had two problems. First, I wasn't in workout clothes. I would look out of place in the gym and would not be very comfortable—literally and socially—doing exercises in this clothing. Second, I was dealing with a fractured finger, and most exercises I do involve gripping barbell weights, which I couldn't do well with my injured finger. These were wonderful excuses.

For the old me, this was a classic "exercise another time" situation. But I had changed. I realized it didn't make a lot of sense to exercise in the situation, but I also thought about the fact that it's a good idea to exercise whenever you can. With this understanding, I committed to an imperfect workout of lunges, tricep dips, and open-handed chest flys. My acceptance of this "unimpressive" workout resulted in quality exercise despite the imperfect situation (note: lunges are intense).

The perfectionist in me saw two strong reasons not to go to the gym. The *imperfectionist* in me saw an opportunity for a little bit of forward progress, and I took it. What some fail to realize is that life is composed of these small decisions. We think that the big decisions, such as "I'm going to lose weight" and "I've decided to write a book," matter most just because they're significant if accomplished. But look back over your life, and think of all the thousands of little moments in which you had an opportunity to be doing something that could have added up to mastery in an area by now. These small everyday decisions (and omissions) form the bulk of our lives.

To continue the transition from mini habits to imperfectionism, let's go deeper into the connection they share. Mini habits are tools of the imperfectionist. They are too small for a perfectionist to appreciate. But they *are* nonthreatening enough that a perfectionist might consider giving them a try. Therefore, mini-habit-based solutions will be integrated heavily into this book.

You Know You're a Perfectionist

In doing research to write books, I like to look at reviews of similar books, especially reviews of three stars and below. Critical reviews highlight what people wished a book would have been or contained. This is not necessarily the author's fault, but it gives insight into *what else* people are seeking.

Readers seemed to have a common frustration with perfectionism books: authors spend too much time telling them signs that they are perfectionists without focusing enough on concrete solutions to *fix* the problem. I recognize that most people who struggle with perfectionism already know they do (buying a book about perfectionism is a good sign of that). That said, it remains important for us to cover the *topic* of perfectionism to understand it. Any problem must be thoroughly understood before it can be fixed, especially one as complex as perfectionism.

In my research, I found two sorts of books on perfectionism. There are the books that play your emotions like a harp, attempting to *woo* you away from perfectionism. Then there are the science-driven books, which pound you with data until you decide that being a perfectionist seems more fun than reading the rest of the book. The better ones combined the two approaches, but I didn't find a book that offered the right solutions. My aim with this book—as with everything I create—is to find the intersection of entertainment and education, practicality and imagination, and to, above all, create a guide that makes lasting change feasible.

~~I'm trying to make this book perfect.~~

Guide: The Journey to Imperfectionism

The most important thing about this book's structure is that the solutions and application are all in the last chapter. In the first nine chapters, we'll discuss concepts in detail to understand them. In the last chapter, I've gathered, categorized, and summarized all the actionable solutions for application. This will make the book very easy to reference quickly.

I want to warn you about this, because otherwise, you might perceive the early parts of the book as a long ramble lacking in practical suggestions. It's structured this way so that you can enjoy the material without having to worry about remembering the solutions and wondering how to apply them to your life. You will find some suggestions before the final chapter, but they won't be fully unpacked until the end.

This is a logical structure because understanding and application are two separate processes. First, we understand and see the big picture, and then we transform that big-picture understanding into something applicable.

Here's the chapter-by-chapter journey to imperfectionism:

Chapter 1: In the introduction, we'll examine perfectionism: What is it? How does it work? Why does it exist, and what purpose does it serve us?

Chapter 2: Second, we'll dive deeper into the perfectionist's mind to identify common thought patterns and the underlying reasons that people are perfectionistic.

Chapter 3: We'll explore the downsides of perfectionism to establish reasons to change.

Chapter 4: Here, we'll take a look at imperfectionism and how it can give us the type of freedom every person craves. Then, we'll have a thorough understanding of why we're perfectionists and why we're better off as imperfectionists. The chapter will end with general solutions for perfectionism.

Chapters 5–9: Perfectionism is a large, branching concept, and so it must be broken down into specific solutions. Five subsets of perfectionism will be dissected one at a time with ideas of how to overcome them. Adopting the general imperfectionist mindset can help—and this is why it's discussed in Chapter 4—but in order to enact significant change for the better, you may need to target your specific flavor(s) of perfectionism with customized solutions. This targeted advice goes well beyond saying, "Don't try to be perfect."

Chapter 10: To conclude, we'll translate all the book's conclusions into actionable mini-habit solutions and, most importantly, give you a framework for how to incorporate them into your life without feeling overwhelmed. Perfectionists in particular struggle to implement good advice because they want to implement it all at once.

Many books will give you 300 pieces of great advice, scatter these randomly throughout the book, and leave you wondering how to apply 300 changes to your life in one night. Hint: it can't be done! Implementation is the hardest part of personal growth, as we always have more on our wish list than we can obtain, so I think you'll find the final chapter and book structure highly useful.

Along the way, I'll do my best not to put you to sleep. If I fail, there's always coffee.

Chapter 1

Introduction

"To be yourself in a world that is constantly trying to make you something else is the greatest accomplishment."

~ Ralph Waldo Emerson

"When the Japanese mend broken objects, they aggrandize the damage by filling the cracks with gold. They believe that when something's suffered damage and has a history it becomes more beautiful."

~ Barbara Bloom

Functional Perfectionists

In the most accurate, technical, and literal sense of the word, a pure perfectionist is someone who is completely dysfunctional in the real world. If you're raising your hand and nodding right now, you're likely to be exaggerating, as most of us are functional as perfectionists but don't live optimally because of it.

- Do you ever struggle to make decisions? Perfectionism.
- Do you ever get intimidated by social situations? Perfectionism.
- Do you ever procrastinate? Perfectionism.
- Do you get depressed easily? (Likely) perfectionism.
- Do you have low self-esteem? Perfectionism.

Perfectionism causes some of life's worst mental problems because it makes life's imperfections into bothersome, intimidating, and unsurpassable roadblocks. Perfectionists are driven mad or frozen in place by the chasm between desire and reality, which impairs their ability to progress and enjoy life. Only imperfectionists can tolerate imperfection, which is the defining attribute of our world.

Thankfully, perfectionism isn't a permanent characteristic. We are capable of changing ourselves, but only with the right strategies. In order to find the right strategies for perfectionism, we must explore the roots of the problem.

"I'm Such a Perfectionist"

We've all either said or heard someone say, "I'm *such* a perfectionist." Have you noticed that people declare it as a flaw yet secretly take some pride in it? People typically smile and laugh as they say it. It's widely seen as a "positive flaw," making it a favorite answer to a despised interview question: "What's your greatest weakness?"

Perfectionists desire to act, look, and/or feel perfect. On a superficial level, it seems like something to be proud of, but not when you dig into the true implications of it. When you add "ism" to the end of "perfection" and "imperfection" to turn them into concepts, the natural connotations of the root words are reversed. Far from perfect, perfectionism is irrational, crippling, restrictive, and even lethal (e.g., anorexia and depression/suicide).

If we fully grasped the reality of perfectionism's destructive influence on humanity, we would not be so eager and happy to label ourselves as perfectionists. I don't judge anyone for it, as we're all perfectionistic in some way, but the phrase "I'm such a perfectionist" is a gaping wound that's commonly treated as a beauty accessory.

This detail matters. Do you know why? Even if you see the freedom and power of imperfectionism after reading this book, it may not be enough. **If you don't manage to reframe perfectionism as a damaging and inferior mindset, the illusion of its superiority will thwart your desired changes.**

Perfectionism causes other serious problems that are commonly diagnosed as something else. For example, it is a very common root cause of depression, which can then lead to a host of other problems such as addictions.

The poster child of perfectionism is anorexia: the desire to reach the "perfect weight" or body image. It's one of the most dangerous and difficult mental disorders to treat. Let's not treat perfectionism casually then. Perfectionism is a disorder of the mind. You'll find that this book is generally lighthearted, but perfectionism is treated too casually by too many, so it had to be said. We've got to stop this secret affinity for perfectionism to be free of it.

Perfectionism is an imposter—a hoax; it's the worst mindset you can pick out of a hat. Imperfectionism, however, is the real deal; it's luxury… five stars… the best. As you read along, seek to develop new mental relationships with these words. Maybe you'll start saying, "I'm *such* an imperfectionist!"

The Science of Perfectionism

Before trying to communicate a useful way to become an imperfectionist, it's necessary for us to untangle perfectionism and examine the individual parts of it. Knowing what a car is and does doesn't mean you can build one, just as knowing what perfectionism is and does doesn't mean you know how to control it. This is why we need to examine it in detail.

Excellent groundwork has been laid for us to understand perfectionism. The problem that remains is a lack of consensus about exactly how to slice and dice perfectionism (as you'll see).

The Research on Perfectionism
In 1990, Professor Randy Frost developed what is called the Frost Multidimensional Perfectionism Scale (FMPS).[2] Here are Frost's six subscales with their common abbreviations:

- Concern over Mistakes (CM)
- Personal Standards (PS)
- Parental Expectations (PE)
- Parental Criticism (PC)
- Doubts about Actions (DA)
- Organization (OR)

(In 1998, Professor Joachim Stoeber suggested these could be simplified and cut down to just four, but he noted that some study results "may indicate that the original FMPS subscales do measure important distinctions, at least in clinical samples.")[3]

In 1991, Hewitt and Gordon Flett came up with the Multidimensional Perfectionism Scale. The scale consisted of 45 items categorized according to the *source* of perfectionism[4]:

- Self-oriented: "unrealistic standards and perfectionistic motivation for the self"
- Other-oriented: "unrealistic standards and perfectionistic motivations for others"
- Socially-prescribed: "the belief that significant others expect oneself to be perfect"

What would happen if someone combined these models? In 2004, researchers from Appalachian State University took these two perfectionism scales, analyzed them, conducted their own studies, and created a new model comprising the following eight subsets of perfectionism organized under two main categories[5]:

Conscientious Perfectionism
- Organization
- Striving for excellence
- Planfulness
- High standards for others

Self-Evaluative Perfectionism
- Concern over mistakes
- Need for approval
- Perceived parental pressure
- Rumination

This is a complex tree of ideas stemming from a single word. You get the sense that none of the scales are perfectly accurate in regard to enveloping the concept of perfectionism. Researchers have been modeling perfectionism, looking to define the word and the problems it causes rather than to form solutions based on this information. That's not a criticism. Their purpose isn't to speculate about solutions as much as it is to say, "This is what we found."

We're not going to enter into the argument of what perfectionism technically is and is not. *We're here to find solutions to a problem.* The question I'm (always) interested in is: "What's the most logical thing to do with this information?"

I've analyzed and narrowed down what I believe are the five most important areas of perfectionism in terms of how "core" they are to the concept and how "fixable" they are. When we start throwing imperfect punches at perfectionism, these will be our targets (in the order they appear in the book and with their sources in parentheses):

- Unrealistic expectations (my addition)
- Rumination (Hill)
- Need for approval (Hill)
- Concern over mistakes (Frost)
- Doubts about actions (Frost)

I left out the "good" forms of perfectionism, such as striving for excellence and organization, because they're not problems and don't need to be solved. And personally, I wouldn't even classify them as perfectionism, but we'll get to that later.

Some subsets were left out for the sake of simplicity and consolidation. For example, parental-related perfectionism is derivative of unrealistic expectations and the need for approval; the solutions aren't any different just because the problem stems from one's parents. Now let's look at the mind of a perfectionist to see whether we can find out why so many people think this way.

Chapter 2

The Perfectionist Mind

"If you look for perfection, you'll never be content."

~ Leo Tolstoy

The Three Types of Perfectionistic Standards

Perfectionism is like ice cream: You can have a large variety of unique flavors, but its base is always milk and sugar. While it's hard to describe all facets of perfectionism completely and concisely, it's possible to discuss its general properties. In this chapter, we'll examine perfectionism broadly.

People abide by three types of perfect standards: context, quality, and quantity.

Perfect Context

This type of perfectionism reduces the number of situations in which a person will take action. Let's use the example of exercise to see how context can be broken down further.

1. Location: Where we're located naturally has a lot to do with our actions. That said, a determined individual would find a way to work out at church, at a party, or on a road trip. Those are examples of places we'd never think to work out, and yet, it wouldn't be too difficult. In the car, you could put your hands down beside you and push your body weight up. You could tense your abdominal muscles. You could bring your knees up and down in your seat. If you wanted to forgo your seat belt (not recommended), you'd have many more options! My family used to do jumping jacks at rest areas when we took road trips.

2. Time of day: Are you only willing to exercise before 4 P.M.? If so, this reduces your options considerably, especially if you have a 9–5 job, in which case you would only be willing to exercise before or during work. Though I don't think it's ideal to exercise at 9 P.M., I've never regretted doing it, because a nonideal 9 P.M. workout is better than not exercising at all.

3. Resources: Without certain resources, some people will refuse to take action. Are you only willing to exercise with gym equipment and in workout clothes? The only exercise equipment you need is your body, unless you're a perfectionist.

Perfect Quality

This is the type of perfectionism that everyone knows and thinks about. People who have this kind of perfectionism are driven mad by their incessant desire for flawless quality. This is most often seen in the workplace, but can also be a big part of family life—for example, if someone won't tolerate less-than-perfect cleanliness or school grades.

Perfect Quantity

Perfectionism by quantity means not being satisfied with an action if it falls below a number threshold. If you asked me how many people I thought struggled with perfectionism, I'd say 95% of the world does, and it's because they aim for perfect quantities.

People seem to think of perfectionism mostly in the sense of quality: getting your hair perfect, having a perfect social interaction, and keeping your desk spotless. The perfectionist mind, however, has a more damaging trick than quality or context, and it's so universally accepted that it evades our radar—perfectly sized accomplishments. This part of perfectionism hasn't been adequately addressed because it's not obvious that goal size is one of the strongest indicators of perfectionism.

Nearly everyone is unknowingly trained to be perfectionists by copying the goal size of the people around them. Every single "normal" goal is perfectionistic in terms of quantity, and almost all people have such goals: lose 30 pounds in six months, write a book this year, make six figures per year, read one book per week, and so on. These aren't impossible goals, but they're perfectionistic because they imply that smaller progress isn't good enough. When I was a perfectionist, my workouts had to be at least 20 (and preferably 30) minutes long; anything less wasn't enough.

A goal is like pole vaulting: Failure is anything underneath the bar, and success is anything above it. It doesn't matter how high you get; it only matters if you get over the bar. This polarized view of goals is supposed to motivate us to reach the mark and maybe even surpass it, but it's an inferior strategy that worsens the perfectionism problem.

How many people have you known to brag about doing three push-ups? Why isn't there a website for people who want to have 30% less debt? What popular exercise program promises to upgrade you from poor to below-average shape?

These all represent meaningful progress, but in your lifetime, you're not likely to encounter *any* of these. We make the grave error of redefining partial success as "failure." If it isn't whole and complete, we find it embarrassing at best and humiliating at worst. This isn't merely irrational—it's lethal to our progress and well-being! **Perfectionists do not accept a small amount of value or progress; they only want big, smooth, perfect wins.**

Large goal size with a clear success and failure line is widespread. Perfectionism is an extreme, so something so "normal" doesn't seem like it could be perfectionism. Well, in this case, the extreme *is* the norm.

Perfectly sized achievements are the most subversive form of perfectionism because you can't and won't fix a problem you don't know about. People are *expected* to set goals to lose 30, 50, or even 100 pounds or more. Nobody considers others "perfectionists" for using such arbitrary large numbers as targets. When we fail to reach those goals, it triggers emotions such as guilt and shame, and we relapse into our old selves.

This section has been a look into the types of perfectionistic standards that permeate our world. This is *what* perfectionism is, so it's time to look at *why*. Next, we'll look at some of the underlying reasons that drive us to perfectionism.

The Precursors of Perfectionism

Perfectionism can be a symptom-producing symptom of some other problem. Let's explore four roots of perfectionism.

Insecurity
Those who are secure in themselves are less perfectionistic because they have a positive affirmation bias, which means they'll assume good things about themselves before considering negative things. A crude example: they might see 5/10 accuracy at the gun range as hitting the target five times instead of missing it five times. Imperfectionists don't focus on their flaws as much as perfectionists do.

When I was a teenager, I had terrible, terrible acne. One kid teased me about my "beard" because of the number of pimples on my chin (he was a wonderful, upstanding gentleman). I was the fifth most self-conscious person on Earth because of it. Later in my life when my skin had cleared up, I met some people with severe acne who were absolutely confident and comfortable with themselves, and it blew my mind. It showed me that I didn't have to be insecure just because I had a highly visible flaw. There was no rule saying I had to be self-conscious because my skin wasn't perfect.

If you're insecure about something, know that there is someone out there who is living confidently and living well in spite of it. That's comforting and empowering.

Inferiority Complex

Google Dictionary defines an inferiority complex as "an unrealistic feeling of general inadequacy caused by actual or supposed inferiority in one sphere, sometimes marked by aggressive behavior in compensation."

Generally speaking, someone who has an inferiority complex reacts in one of two ways—they try hard to be perceived as *superior* (in reality or appearance), or they clam up. These are logical responses to an illogical perspective. If you truly believe that you're worse than other people, it only makes sense to act like a threatened puffer fish (intimidate) or turtle (hide).

The less you think of yourself, the more likely you are to overcompensate. If you have an aggressive or extroverted personality, your inferiority complex will usually result in the puffer fish response. If you have a passive, shy personality, this usually results in the turtle response.

The less you think of yourself, the harder you'll be on yourself. Inferiority complexes create a powerful negative affirmation bias; every blunder is magnified evidence that confirms your feelings, and every misstep is a catastrophe. Insecurity and inferiority complexes alike make you hypersensitive to your flaws. Holding on to this idea that if you're careful you won't make mistakes gives a false sense of security. The only real security is knowing and accepting who you are right now. If you embrace your identity with your flaws included, it's a powerful defense against even the harshest criticism. Otherwise, the image you present to the world is like a turtle shell, and the real you is underneath, naked, vulnerable, and afraid.

To think yourself inferior to any person requires you to evaluate yourself or others unfairly: Either you see other people as mostly perfect beings without problems (ha!), or you see yourself as being a worse-than-average person (or some combination of both). If you overestimate others, you'd have to be perfect just to meet their level. If you see yourself as subpar, you'd have to be perfect just to seem average in your own eyes. It all works out the same in that an inferiority complex is based on unfair standards and a warped view of humanity, and it makes you act like a perfectionist.

Discontentment

When you don't like your life, your risk of perfectionism goes up considerably. It's not that all perfectionists dislike their lives, but those who dislike their lives often become perfectionists. It's a counterintuitive truth:

when you wish things were better, it's tempting to pretend and insist that they already are. Those who are discontent are most likely to pretend they're *perfectly content.*

Facing reality, facing flaws, and owning up to an imperfect existence is not easy. It's a skill that some people never learn. And here's an interesting question: who is to blame for those who don't develop the ability to tolerate imperfection? Some studies have found a connection between parenting style and perfectionism in kids. While parents demanding perfection from their kids is an obvious first exposure to this mindset, I don't think it's fair to place all the blame on them. Formal education can be a cause too.

School

Grades are used to gauge how well a student is learning; this isn't an inherently bad idea, but it becomes one as the entire focus of school becomes getting those perfect "A"s. And while a "C" is supposed to represent an average grade, the perception for many students and parents is that "A"s are the only acceptable grade and anything less is disappointing. Does this sound familiar? It's just like how most people set goals. School grades and perfect goals stem from the assumption that the ideal result (e.g., getting an "A" or losing 50 pounds) is also the ideal aim.

In addition, school teaches us that "'A' efforts" bring "'A' results." Real life shows us that "'A' efforts" only give us a *chance* at "'A' results." Students can go out into the job market, do all the right things, and still get a real-life "F" when they aren't selected for a job. This is the ideal breeding ground for perfectionistic thinking.

These issues have the common impact of making us afraid and uncertain. All negative behaviors and mindsets, including perfectionism, provide some type a benefit that draws people to them. Based on the common impact of the factors discussed, can you guess the primary benefit of perfectionism?

The Benefit of Perfectionism (Perceived Safety)

Perfectionism is an excuse-generating machine. After setting a perfect standard, attempting to meet it seems futile. Such a standard can also be a *response* to underlying fears and doubts. For example, if I feared that I couldn't write well, I might then create an irrationally high standard for my writing to discourage myself from ever attempting to write—for example, *my first draft must be as concise as Hemingway and as witty as Shakespeare.* This would prevent me from writing a single word!

The perfectionist enjoys safety and protection from what they fear, and that—not striving for excellence—is the most common reason why people become perfectionists. This is clearly seen because of *when* we are the most perfectionistic. Have you noticed that the higher the stakes (and fear), the more perfectionistic a person will be?

Most people aren't as concerned with being praised as much as they are about preventing embarrassment. Author and researcher Brené Brown says that perfectionism is a 20-ton shield we carry around in hopes that it protects us from harm. "In truth," she says, "what it does is keep us from being seen."[6] If you're unseen, you can't be embarrassed, but does anyone really want to remain unseen? Being seen and even embarrassed occasionally is an essential part of life.

The Illusion of Greatness

Desire for greatness and fear of inadequacy are counterforces, and perfectionism is the only solution that *seems* to address both. You can fantasize about greatness while remaining protected against embarrassment. Inaction, in this case, even appears to validate your great potential because desiring perfection implies that you have and can meet high standards (when you run out of excuses), but it only hides your potential from yourself and the world.

If perfectionism were an iceberg, the small, visible tip would be a desire for excellence, and the submerged part, which reportedly comprises 90% of an iceberg's mass, would be the fear of failure. The fear of failure is not something we want to show to the world, but it can still drive our actions.

There is yet another caveat to this perplexing mindset that I want to make clear: it's not the literal consequences of failure that scare us; it's the idea that we could fail at something we desire greatly.

We cling to perfectionism not because the cost of failure rises but because the importance of the reward rises. The more we want something, the more afraid we are to not get it. A "perfect" example of this is one of the many low-risk and high-reward behaviors that trigger a perfectionistic response in people: asking a girl to go on a date, asking for a raise, meeting new people, or trying something new. Each of these usually has a negligible downside compared to the great upside if it's a success. Why then, would they trigger this response? Failure has two components to it.

The Two Considerations of Failure

The first, most obvious component of failure is the literal impact of failing. If you fail to jump across a ravine, you'll get gravely hurt or killed by falling into it. But failure in the examples given in the previous paragraph come with little to no consequences. You might feel slightly worse and less confident because of rejection, but you'll be no worse off in most cases.

The reason we can still be fearful of these near-zero risk actions is the second component of failure—meaning and symbolism. If you fail to do something, you will naturally wonder why. Why did she say no? Why didn't I get the raise? Am I unintelligent because I couldn't complete a Rubik's cube on my first or tenth try?

The answer to these bigger questions is what we fear the most. Your boss said you couldn't get a raise. Why? You might think it's because you're not good enough, you don't have what it takes, and your career has hit its ceiling. Suddenly, this zero-risk attempt has thrown a knockout punch to your confidence and self-esteem!

We fear what failure *means* about who we are. We fear that it will expose our weaknesses and damage our vulnerable hopes and dreams. That's scary stuff! I used to be a perfectionist in fearing this type of "symbolic failure" with women. *If one woman rejects me, so will the rest!*

Perfectionism protects us against symbolic failure. Because low-risk and high-reward opportunities are often tied to concepts that we crave success in—romance, career, and socializing—an individual instance of failure can be seen as symbolic of our standing in that area, even though, logically, it's more of a chance-based result than a life-defining failure. (We'll cover this more in the second half of the book.)

In this dynamic is another "benefit" of perfectionism—mystery! If you never attempt something, you can't know empirically that you're not world-class at it. The mystery in perfectionism allows our perfect fantasies to never be tested and disproved. A quick logic check tells us that *we're not perfect at anything.* So there's not actually any mystery; it's just the illusion of it.

It's important to be honest about this—*perfectionism does protect us*. It protects us from massively damaging our confidence and hopes. (Otherwise, it wouldn't be so popular.) Being a perfectionist *seems* prudent and responsible based on this perspective.

To this, I have a potentially life-changing question for you to consider: do you want or *need* this type of protection?

Being protected is not always best for us. Consider animals that grow up protected in shelters and so lack the skills to survive in the wild. Consider individual muscle fibers, which are torn through exercise and then built back stronger. Protection often weakens that which it protects.

Perfectionism significantly weakens us over time by making us overprotective against mistakes and failures that carry a short-term downside and a long-term upside. The idea is as follows: **if you can withstand something undesirable AND it strengthens you, you're far better off "unprotected" against it.**

Are You an Overdriven or Paralyzed Perfectionist?

Perfectionists tend to be overdriven or paralyzed and sometimes both.

Overdriven perfectionists are never satisfied. It's not just that they're striving for better and better things, but that they're never happy with what they have and what they or others have done.

Paralyzed perfectionists are those who let the fear of failure trap them into living a less meaningful life. They'll play it safe by doing things like watching TV, only doing what they're "supposed to do," and taking very few risks.

Those who are overdriven struggle the most with **unrealistic expectations** and **rumination**. Those who are paralyzed struggle the most with **concern over mistakes** and **doubts about actions**. Both types tend to struggle somewhat with the **need for approval**, which can push someone into hiding or into extreme effort. Both types can struggle with any of these five subsets, which we'll cover in the solutions half of the book.

In this chapter, we've gained an understanding of what perfectionism is and what it does for us. In the next chapter, we're going to uncover some of the more sinister consequences of perfectionism.

Chapter 3

The Poison of Perfectionism

"Striving for excellence motivates you; striving for perfection is demoralizing."

~ Harriet Braiker

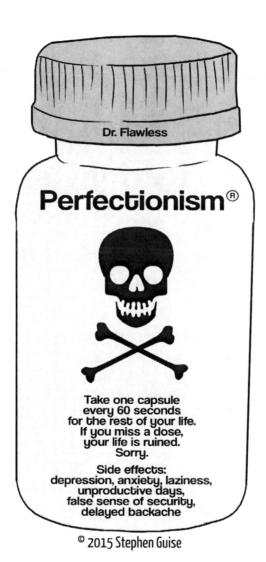

Perfectionism's Toxicity

Initially, I had titled this chapter "The Misery of Perfectionism." But perfectionism does more than make us feel bad; it harms us. Perfectionism works like a poison: If you ingest a mild poison, you might suffer from it but not even be aware of its negative effects because you're used to the symptoms. The poison of perfectionism can remain undetected in smaller doses, subtly impairing your life; in larger doses, it can be lethal to your well-being.

It may also be lethal in a literal sense. A study on 450 elderly participants found that those with perfectionistic tendencies were 51% more likely to die in the course of the six and a half year study.[7] Other studies have found perfectionism to be strongly linked to higher rates of depression and suicide,[8] and that the risk has been underestimated.[9]

One study found perfectionism "to be a primary disruptive factor in the short-term treatment of depression, whether the treatment is pharmacotherapy (imipramine), cognitive-behavior therapy, interpersonal therapy, or placebo."[10] This suggests that depression may not be the condition we should be treating. Maybe we need to focus on the underlying perfectionism mindset that leads so many people to depression and suicidal thoughts.

A mindset's merit is based on how it affects your actions and how you feel about those actions. The perfectionism mindset generally has a negative impact on both of those areas. But are there any aspects of it that are helpful or even healthy?

Is All Perfectionism Bad?

It's my view that the entire concept of perfectionism is bad, but if I'm honest I know it's not that simple. So, if you ask me, "Is all perfectionism bad?" in the way it is currently defined, I have to admit that some aspects of perfectionism are good.

Don Hamacheck may have introduced the concept of healthy perfectionism. He said in 1978 that perfectionism ranged from "normal to neurotic" and that perfectionism in the normal range was healthy. Normal perfectionists, he said, "feel free to be less precise as the situation permits," while neurotic perfectionists "are unable to feel satisfaction because in their own eyes they never seem to do things good enough to warrant that feeling."[11]

How can being "less precise" have anything to do with perfectionism, which rejects less-than-perfect precision by definition? I digress.

Within Frost's Multidimensional Perfectionism Scale (FMPS), researchers and the general public alike commonly see personal standards (PS) and organization (O) as positive forms of perfectionism. Psychologist Thomas Greenspon points out why they may not be:

"What Frost et al. (1990)[12] said, however, is that, while these two subscales reflect several positive personality characteristics, Personal Standards is also significantly correlated with depression, and Organization 'does not appear to be a core component of perfectionism.'"[13]

Personal standards provide positive characteristics and are correlated with depression because they're made from two components: striving for excellence and high expectations. As I'll explain further in the Unrealistic Expectations chapter, these can and should be separated. Striving for excellence, on its own, is wholly good. High expectations are the problem.

Organization is arguably not even a part of perfectionism. Not all researchers agree with the liberties taken with the word. Psychologist Asher Pacht believed perfectionism to be unhealthy in all circumstances.[14] And Greenspon succinctly summarized the problem with so-called "healthy perfectionism" when he wrote: **"People defined as healthy perfectionists are never described as actually seeking perfection."**[15]

That quote is so important. If only the world saw the truth in Greenspon's quote above, we wouldn't be so confused about what perfectionism is. But we are confused, because striving for excellence is an important part of anyone's journey to success. As a result, many people view perfectionism as a "necessary struggle" for success—especially in the arts—and all the damaging aspects we're going to cover in this chapter are thrown in with it. If you believe you must be a perfectionist to achieve things, you're more likely to see excessive self-criticism and other harmful perfectionistic tendencies as normal or even necessary (they're not).

But, as you can see, perfectionism's once-sharp definition has been blurred, and it has penetrated our society. I could fill many pages with quotes from famous people claiming to be perfectionists. Most appear to say to mean they strive for excellence; others are actually describing a self-critical nature; still others say it to denote both. Among dozens of "I'm a perfectionist" quotes that reflect the blurred definition, I could only find two prominent public figures who seem to distinguish perfectionism from striving for excellence.

"People call me a perfectionist, but I'm not. I'm a rightist. I do something until it's right, and then I move on to the next thing."
~ James Cameron, director of the two highest grossing films in history (Titanic and Avatar)

"I'm not a perfectionist. I'm a person who strives for excellence and requires excellence. There is a difference."
~ Oprah Winfrey, talk show host with 10 appearances on the Time 100 list of most influential Americans

Although I would love to change the world's understanding of perfectionism to exclude striving for excellence and organization—which are healthy— most people still include those attributes in their definition. Accepting this, let us at least draw a clear line between harmful perfectionism and helpful perfectionism. I've learned something critical in problem solving and in life: **it's always best to begin where things are, not where you wish they were.** Right now, perfectionism is defined as having these two healthy subsets. And if striving for excellence and organization are widely considered to be parts of perfectionism, then no, perfectionism isn't all bad.

Usually, it's the drop of poison that spoils the bucket of water, but in this case, helpful perfectionism (as some define it) is the drop of water that dilutes the bucket of poisonous perfectionism. Now that we've identified the drop of water, it's time to examine the poison.

Passive Living (Television and Perfectionism)

If you're a perfectionist of the paralyzed sort, it's almost guaranteed that you watch a lot of TV. Perfectionists and procrastinators love TV because nobody watches TV incorrectly. It is completely passive, which makes it an automatic, simple, rewarding, and mistake-free "win." Any passive activity is safe for the perfectionist, because if they're not involved, they can't mess up. I believe perfectionism is the primary reason why Americans watch so much TV every day.

- Ages 18-34 watch TV an average of **4 hours 17 minutes** per day.
- Ages 35-49 watch TV an average of **4 hours 57 minutes** per day.
- Ages 50-64 watch TV an average of **6 hours 12 minutes** per day.[16]

Being sedentary for extended periods of time is lethal,[17] but that only involves the body. The most worrying thing about this data is that Americans are mentally passive for *at least* five hours a day (on average), and increasingly so as we age. That changes it from a lifespan issue to an *Are we even living?* issue.

Physical limitations (such as from injury or old age) are poor excuses for passivity. Jon Morrow is an entrepreneur; he was born with spinal muscular atrophy, which has paralyzed him from the neck down. He has no choice but to sit, and yet he is not passive. Jon makes over $100,000 per month by using his voice.[18]

"I would rather die doing what I want to do than die in a nursing home bed somewhere watching TV for 15 hours a day, surrounded by other people waiting to die. To me, that is the scariest thing imaginable."
~ Jon Morrow

If there were ever a *valid* excuse to do nothing but watch TV, it'd probably be something like, "I'm paralyzed from the neck down." Jon has taken that one off the table. I am not criticizing anyone for watching TV. TV is not the enemy—it is merely a symptom of a bigger problem. If your perfectionistic mindset makes you want to procrastinate and escape your life, TV is going to be hard to resist. These numbers are high, but not surprising, because most people are perfectionists!

One assumed benefit of perfectionism is that, for all its problems, at least it'll help you perform better, right? Some research suggests that this may not be the case.

Perfectionism Can Hurt Performance

You'll find this study interesting: Using Frost's perfectionism scale, 51 undergraduate women were tested to determine their level of perfectionism. Afterward, they were tasked with rewording a passage as concisely as possible without losing any of its meaning. Then, two college professors (who were unaware of the students' perfectionism scores and thus impartial) graded their papers. Those who tested high in perfectionism wrote passages that "were judged significantly poorer in quality than subjects low in perfectionism."[19]

Though the study had a small sample size, the difference between the two groups was found to be *significant.* A plausible explanation would be that the less perfectionist students practiced writing more often (perfectionism, not a lack of ideas, is the one and only cause of writer's block), thus building up a stronger writing skill set. Another explanation is that perfectionism turns up your conscious intensity dial to extreme levels, to the point that it interferes with subconscious operations; this can have a negative impact on creativity, focus, and subconscious-driven activities.

When I play basketball, I'm usually relaxed and having fun. At other times, I find myself concerned about playing perfectly. Anyone who plays sports knows the difference between the two mindsets, and they'll all—including me —tell you that they play better when they're relaxed. But why is this?

The best results in sports and in life come from training. When trained in something to the point that it's second nature (and subconscious), your conscious mind can relax, and a relaxed mind is more effective and useful than a tense mind because it can focus more easily.

It's strange to think that perfectionists would ever perform worse. The problem lies in trying to run a mistake-free program (those are incompatible with the human operating system). This makes perfectionism even less attractive, because improved performance is supposed to be its one redeeming quality.

We all want to perform well, not poorly. To that effect, perfectionists have a technique called "self-handicapping" to allow for the possibility of success while discrediting their failures. This sounds nice, but self-handicapping comes at a cost.

Self-Handicapping Holds Us Back

Have you ever seen someone lose and immediately serve up a ready-made platter of excuses as to why they lost? I've done it before.

There's a term called "self-handicapping" that describes how people purposefully handicap themselves—explicitly or mentally—to have an excuse on hand if things don't work out. When done explicitly, it might be letting someone get a head start in a race because if you give them a head start and they win, you can say it's because they started first. If self-handicapping mentally, you may start the race from the same spot, but in your head, you'll think, "My knee hurts and I'm tired" instead of "I'm going to win this race."

We do this to protect ourselves. It seems nice, too, to have a chance of success but to say, "Well, my ankle was sore" if the attempt fails. It is riskier to accept the full consequences of an action.

Self-handicapping is a perfectionist trait in that it lets you put an asterisk beside your failures, but it's also a hindrance to success. It's playing life safely instead of playing to win. I can't tell you how many football teams I've seen lose in the fourth quarter only because they played it safe and let the other team methodically storm back. Of course, some have still won the game by playing it safe, just as some people still win with self-handicapping, but if you've ever seen a team *not* let up, it's hard to argue that playing it safe is the best way.

When the New England Patriots of the National Football League (NFL) build a lead, they continue to play to win instead of playing not to lose. It's coach Bill Belichick's strategy to continue to score points. Because of this, they have been accused several times of "running up the score," denoted by playing for more points when the game is clearly won. It seems to work well for them, because as of writing, they have an NFL-best 72 straight victories when leading at the half.[20]

I know it's cliché, but life is too short to play it safe. Given our natural limit of about 100 years, we have every reason to throw ourselves at the world with a good measure of (smart) reckless abandon. That's the mark of the imperfectionist. It won't be satisfying at the end of your life to have solid excuses for not doing all the things you wanted to do.

In life, you're consistently building up one of two things—your level of comfort or your level of growth. To grow in an area, you must face increased risk, uncertainty, and discomfort. There is absolutely no other option, because if growth were comfortable, then you'd already be at that point. Does that make sense? Let me give you a tangible example.

Let's say that I want to get physically stronger. In order to do this, I have to get uncomfortable. I have to lift somewhat heavy weights, which is challenging on a mental and physical level. I'll feel physical discomfort as my body strains to push or pull the weight. Mentally, the best way I can describe weight lifting is that it's annoying; my mind pesters me: "Stephen, put the weight down and go play video games!"

Weight lifting breaks down muscle fiber in much the same way that we're "broken down" when we fail or go through an uncomfortable experience. And just as a muscle is built back stronger, so are we as a result of the lessons we learn by attempting something and failing. **This is not a cheap platitude; neurologically, our brains become more resilient to whatever failures and discomfort we experience regularly.** Think about the guy who has been turned down for 200 dates versus the guy who has never been turned down. Who will take the next rejection better? The guy whose brain already knows the process.

It's interesting to look at the most skilled people in various professions and think, *She used to be terrible at this,* and *He used to be unskilled at that.* The road to excellence begins unimpressively. I think we all know this, but I don't think we realize how much we subconsciously avoid this rocky path through self-handicapping, which attempts to simulate a smooth upward path. No such path exists. We try to come up with an excuse for every stumble instead of simply accepting that we stumble sometimes and can get back up.

Think about some of the important areas in your life right now—school, business, career, fitness, romance, social life, and so on. Do you self-handicap in these areas? If so, you value them. We only self-handicap when we care. For example, we have no need to seriously self-handicap when ordering a meal: "I would have gotten the fish tacos, but my, uh, glasses were foggy." If you order the wrong thing, it doesn't matter, because it's just one meal. (Note: some people may still take a long time to order or may comment about getting the wrong dish, but it won't be because of self-handicapping.)

Areas that people self-handicap in include the following:

- Business and career success (e.g., putting in a halfhearted effort at work or slacking on your business, almost as if you're "saving" your best work for a special occasion or the right moment)
- Romance (e.g., not investing in or pursuing relationships, being emotionally distant, etc.)
- Social situations (e.g., finding reasons to avoid conversations, pretending not to care, etc.)
- Personal appearance (e.g., not presenting your best self, because if people reject a lesser version of you, you'll have an excuse)
- Personal health (e.g., not exercising because you have a minor injury or health concern; you can almost always exercise around it!)

Let's be driven, passionate-for-life people who don't hold back, because tomorrow isn't a given. Self-handicapping is derived from perfectionism, and its flavor of poison is prepackaged excuses that let us live inferior lives when we could be thriving, stumbling, getting back up, and thriving again.

Perfectionism is clearly a problem, but it isn't an immediate fix. It's rooted in habit.

The Perfectionism Habit: "Perfect Is Adequate"

Our subconscious creates patterns of behavior—habits—that comprise roughly 45% of our lives (according to the results of a Duke University journal study).[21] Some habits are externally visible: going to the gym, smoking cigarettes, eating an apple for breakfast each morning, and touching your face when nervous. Others, such as habitual thought patterns, are not visible or obvious in our actions.

Perfectionism is one such "invisible" habit. It's a systematic way of thinking that says, "Perfect is adequate." You can see the problem with this equation. Perfect and adequate are not supposed to be equals. If perfect is your version of adequate, then life won't ever seem adequate, let alone good.

Your floor and ceiling are important considerations in life. Your floor in this case is the absolute minimum you need to be satisfied in life. Your ceiling is your upper potential and wildest dreams. If you're living in between your floor and your ceiling, you're happy, because you have the minimum of what you need to be happy. And it goes without saying that you won't surpass your ceiling (or else it isn't a ceiling).

Perfectionism is a problem because it makes "perfection" your floor. When this is the case, you don't have a ceiling. *The floor is also the ceiling because perfection can't be surpassed!* This setup seems cramped even to me, and I live in a 150-square-foot "micro studio" apartment!

Perfectionists are prone to thinking this way, but what must be understood is the habitual root that drives it. Because perfectionism is a habitual way of perceiving the world, change must be approached neurologically, not with "you can do it" sentiments.

How Can We Change?

Let's set aside the topic of perfectionism for a moment to tackle a serious and relevant issue: How do we change? The ultimate goal of this book is to help you become an imperfectionist, but this book approaches change differently from most. The books that tell you to "be free" and "let go" without any kind of concrete, actionable strategy are of questionable (at best) value. They'll make you feel good, but if your brain doesn't change, neither do you. I won't say it's impossible to achieve lasting change based on a motivational spark from such a book, but it's unlikely.

If you come to this book having read *Mini Habits*, you're already familiar with the problem of using motivation as a strategy for taking action, and you may be tempted to skim this section. There is, however, some new information in this section that wasn't in *Mini Habits*, and it'd be a good idea to review it anyway because it's important. It explains why the solutions (which start in the last section of the next chapter) will be converted into action-first mini habits for application.

Is Motivation Enough?

The most popular approach to change is fatally flawed because it's a "flash in the pan" strategy and transformation doesn't happen quickly. As mentioned in *Mini Habits*, for a lasting change to occur, the brain must have enough repetition over time to form new neural pathways. If this doesn't happen, your brain and behavior will revert to their old ways.

Have you ever tried to "get motivated" to do something positive in your life? If I were to form a single phrase to describe "getting motivated," it would be *emotional manipulation*. You currently feel "blah" about doing something but want to feel "rah rah" about it so that you'll want to do it. For many tasks, this means thinking about the benefits until you want to take action.

Whatever the means, the goal is to change the way you *feel* about the behavior. This is desirable, because if you get yourself to want to do something, it's easy, feels natural, and doesn't require willpower. It isn't smart, though, because it doesn't *always* work. In the case of books about perfectionism, encouraging readers with sentiments of "You are good enough" or "Your work is good enough" could temporarily quell the domineering grasp of perfectionism on their minds and make them feel empowered, but it's not a lasting solution.

"Getting motivated" begins in the mind. To better understand why this is the wrong place to begin, let's talk about how emotions, motivation, action, and habits relate to each other.

Emotions, Motivation, Action, and Habits

Emotions motivate us to take action, but the reverse is also true: emotions follow action. Actions make us feel, and feelings make us act. While most of the world focuses on the fact that feeling can cause doing, fewer think about how doing can cause feeling, which can then cause more doing.

For example, imagine a husband and wife who are in love. They feel strongly for each other, and these feelings make them want to kiss each other. This is the flow we see most: emotions into action.

There's a story of a husband who tells his wife he wants a divorce because he doesn't love her anymore. She's upset, but before she signs the divorce papers, she requests that he carry her from their bedroom to the front door every morning, as he had carried her into her bridal room on their wedding day. He laughs at the odd request and agrees. But as the days go on, this act of carrying her increases the intimacy he feels for her, their romance is rekindled, and they stay together. According to Snopes.com, this story is a legend,[22] but the concept is true: our actions greatly impact how we feel, and the effect is so powerful that it changes us even if we don't want or mean for it to.

People like to say that love is an action and not an emotion, but it's really both, and they tend to "self-align" with each other. When you act lovingly, you'll feel it more. But when you feel no love, you're not likely to act lovingly. What's the best way to approach this? There are several reasons to believe that starting with action is the best strategy.

In an experiment by social psychologist Amy Cuddy, one group was instructed to assume a high-power pose and another a low-power pose, both for two minutes. The high-power pose group members stood tall and placed their hands on their hips or held their arms out (open, wide, and taking up space). The low-power pose group members folded their arms inward and slouched (closed, confined, and taking up less space).

After just two minutes, the high-power pose group's testosterone levels increased 20%, and their cortisol levels decreased 25%. The high-power group was found to be far more willing to take risks than the low-power posers in subsequent tests. Increased testosterone makes us more willing to take risks and be assertive, while decreased cortisol makes us less anxious and stressed. As for the low-power pose group, their pose had the inverse effect: testosterone dropped 10%, and cortisol increased 15%.[23]

"Two minutes led to these hormonal changes that configure your brain to basically be either assertive, confident, and comfortable, or really stress-reactive and feeling kind of shut down." [24]
~ Amy Cuddy

This is a powerful, scientific piece of evidence that shows how profoundly even simple actions can impact the way we feel on a chemical level! There's even more direct evidence that the action-first strategy is superior in regard to changing how we feel (and increasing motivation). The Duke University journal study mentioned earlier found that emotional change was almost twice as likely to be caused by actions the study participants had taken as opposed to thoughts.[25]

What Changes Our Emotions? (Study Results)

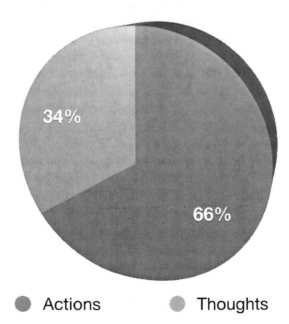

● Actions   ● Thoughts

Now, we were talking about feeling and doing, and this study talks about *thinking* versus doing. **Thinking is the standard way people try to change their feelings in the "get motivated" strategy. They won't try action until they're in a mental and emotional state in which action is attractive to them.**

Another problem: Thoughts are tainted by the very emotions they're attempting to eradicate, which can make emotional change a highly difficult endeavor. This is why people struggle with motivation. If the feeling isn't there, it's not as simple as choosing to get motivated or thinking about your goals. It can work on occasion, but it will not work every time.

It's unfortunate how popular this strategy is, because it's *much* easier to generate motivation by acting first. To a motivation-driven person, this seems invalid based on their flawed premise that we can't take action if we're not motivated to do it. We also have willpower, which grants us the ability to act against our feelings. If action through willpower is something we can do with regularity, then it matches the data as a superior starting point for generating the most motivation and taking more action in an area.

The main point here is that action itself is the best starting point for more action, while trying to think your way into more motivation is an unreliable and ineffective way to create forward momentum. In addition, the "get motivated" strategy assumes that you'll always *want* to get motivated. What if your ultimate goal is motivation to exercise, but after a long day of work, you don't even *want* to be motivated to exercise and thus don't try to increase your motivation? "Getting motivated" is a strategy that attempts to build from a point of weakness. It's better to start with strength.

What could possibly be a strength to build from when you're unmotivated to take action? There isn't much. This is why people get stuck. But you can create a position of strength by using a negligible amount of willpower to take one small step forward or to complete a "mini goal." The basis of *Mini Habits* was to leverage this process into its most potent application—forming habits.

Some will point out that we need at least a small bit of motivation to do *anything* except autonomous functions such as breathing, and this is true. But this is not the type of motivation we've been talking about. Motivation has two meanings that are quite different from each other, and we need only one of the two kinds in order to take action.

The Two Types of Motivation
Did you know that it's possible to be motivated to write a book but not be

motivated to write *in* your book? How? The first motivation means having a general reason and desire to write a book. The second type is moment-by-moment motivation, which varies greatly based on context and your emotional state. I think we can all relate to wanting to do something in general but changing our minds when the time comes for action!

The type of motivation we *don't* need is the type that fluctuates. Its constant fluctuation is exactly what makes it unreliable, and it has no doubt killed some of your goals in the past. If you're the type of person who sets a goal and goes one to six weeks strong with it, only to quit suddenly for various reasons, you're well versed in how fluctuating motivation kills goals.

You'll hear motivation talked about as a single concept because people use their reason to do something as their emotional spark to *feel like doing it*. I'm not doubting the logic of this. It's not a stretch to believe that your reason to fly might motivate you to jump in the pilot seat. It often works. But think about what we just covered.

To rely on the connection between your reason to do something and your current desire to do something means that when you don't feel it, you must *think* about *why* you should write the book, work out, clean your house, or meditate. And yet, the studies above demonstrated the most powerful cross-connection to be between emotions and *action*, as action changed emotions about twice as often as thoughts did. This doesn't *automatically* mean that actions are better, but it probably does.

Consider Cuddy's study that showed how our bodies react chemically to body language. The evidence is all around us that action creates a more powerful and *reliable* emotional response in us than thoughts do. Given that we experience far more thoughts than actions per day and actions still impacted emotions twice as often in the study, it's a good indication that the action-to-emotion connection is stronger.

To think that the motivational idea of *If I have a reason to, desire will eventually follow* works every time is naive and goes against the fickle nature of human feelings. We must not underestimate the power of a bad, anxious, or lazy mood! Let me put it this way: When you treat how you feel as the deciding factor of what you do, you will be a slave to it. You will try so many motivational techniques, but in the end, your results will be as unreliable as your feelings.

All this is fascinating when you consider the rampant popularity of "chasing motivation." According to the sales rankings of best-selling books, motivation is the seventh-most popular nonfiction category and the second-most popular self-help category on Amazon.[26] (There's not even a category for "willpower," "discipline," or "small steps.") This flawed way of thinking is well ingrained in our society. Everywhere you look, people are seeking or teaching motivational techniques, and it genuinely saddens me.

People who have successfully changed their lives have figured out that when you start doing something, your emotions follow suit.

Never forget this: It's easier to change your mind and emotions by taking action than it is to change your actions by trying to think and feel differently.

Do Habits Drain Motivation?

There is another problem with motivation-based action, which is its natural incompatibility with habits. The Texas study mentioned earlier found that people were notably less emotional about habitual behavior than non-habitual behavior. As a behavior is repeated, the subconscious recognizes the pattern, the neural pathway is strengthened, and our emotions toward the behavior decrease. This is intuitive for us, because what's more electrifying than your first kiss? What's more delicious than your first taste of pizza? Or even your first slice of pizza compared to the fourth slice? Repetition is how we learn, but as newness fades, so do our emotions toward it. There are other factors that can cause emotional variation, but all things being equal, habits decrease emotion.

Now, imagine a person riding an emotion-driven wave of motivation, trying to create a habit (such as a New Year's resolution). The further they go toward forming the habit, the weaker the wave will get, until they're left motionless and are then tasked with swimming (using willpower) or quitting. This is a reasonable explanation for why people frequently quit new goals after one to six weeks. At that point in time, the transition to the subconscious is most likely underway just as emotion (and motivation) is waning.

Motivation should more or less be ignored if you want your changes to last. This is not to say that motivation isn't valuable. On the contrary, both forms of it are essential for building a great life. We're strictly talking about starting strategies to consider for our upcoming perfectionism solutions, because having a reliable starting strategy is what enables us to *keep going* with our desired changes.

We just covered why we'll use action-first strategies to apply our perfectionism solutions. There is one more requirement for successful change —targeted solutions. For example, if you did random exercises hoping for a six-pack, you could very well be wasting your time. You need to know what behaviors lead to six-pack abs.

Sustainability tends to be the more difficult part of the equation because solutions are usually obvious: to get in shape, eat healthy food and exercise, and to get good at snowboarding, practice snowboarding. But perfectionism is so abstract and complex that targeted solutions are not immediately obvious. We can't say, "Just don't try to be so perfect!" This is easier said than done, and it is not a *targeted* solution.

In the second half of the book, we'll combine these two factors of change and look at action-first solutions to specific problems of perfectionism. Before we get there, the next chapter will cover the general mindset and freedom that imperfectionism brings. Here is where the fun begins!

Chapter 4

The Freedom of Imperfectionism

"No matter how slow you go, you are still lapping everyone on the couch."

~ Unknown

© 2015 Stephen Guise

No Limits

Imperfectionism is freedom because it's our natural state. It's the way we're born to be. Perfectionism is the artificial construct that constricts, rigidifies, and conforms behavior to an unreasonable standard.

Imperfectionism is NOT laziness, low standards, contentment with failure, disinterest in excellence and improvement, or apathy. At its core, imperfectionism is pursuing and doing good things in life without so much as hoping for (let alone expecting) perfection. It's prioritizing doing over doing well. This doesn't rule out doing things well; *it only takes away the crippling fear of not doing well.*

The premise of imperfectionism—and this is key—is that having lower standards does not equate to getting worse results. A common, false assumption is that aiming for perfection gets you closer to it. The opposite is true: Embracing imperfection will bring you closer to perfection than a perfectionist mindset will. A study referenced earlier showed that perfectionistic students performed considerably worse than others in a writing assignment.

Taking it one step further, accepting imperfection doesn't mean thinking, *Unfortunately, I have to accept this mindset for my well-being.* If you frame imperfection as a necessary evil, it's not going to help you very much. It's better to internalize how and why it's your preferred way to live. The people who thrive are the ones who embrace imperfectionism.

This isn't an isolated, unique "human" discussion; the beauty of imperfection is all around us. For example, diamonds are cut and refined into beautiful stones. But before they're beautiful stones, they're ugly masses of carbon. When carbon is exposed to years of extreme heat and pressure, it forms into a diamond. Think of your effort as being represented by the heat and pressure that make plain ol' carbon into the world's most famous stone. It doesn't merely require a lot of effort; it also requires time and consistency to make yourself into something greater. Perfectionism doesn't work because it's based on the (ironically) flawed notion that great things happen all at once on the first try.

The primary benefits of becoming an imperfectionist are reduced stress and greater results by taking positive action in more situations. The more fearless, confident, and free a person is, the more they embrace imperfection in their life. If you want anything great to happen in your life, you've got to start moving forward now, even if you've got a flat tire, a rusty frame, and a busted headlight. It's only by moving forward that you see new horizons, open up new possibilities, and have more opportunities to grow and enjoy life.

An Imagination Exercise
What would life be like if you fully accepted your insecurities, weaknesses, and mistakes? Use your imagination to *feel* what the freedom of imperfectionism would be like in an area where you've never allowed it. If you can visualize it, you can see the wild appeal of it:

There you are. You're fully aware of all of your problems, but they don't bother you. You find yourself in that one situation in which you are typically perfectionistic, but this version of you is carefree. A few things go wrong, but you react calmly. It's almost annoying how much this version of you doesn't care about being judged, making mistakes, being rejected, making perfect decisions, and getting everything just right. This version of you doesn't get nervous or anxious. You're completely relaxed in a calm, focused, and productive way. You're at a party now, and you flashed some dance moves that nobody had ever seen before. (That took a lot of guts, but you didn't think twice about it.)

Imperfectionists live life to the fullest. And while imperfectionists are generally loved for unabashedly being themselves, they tend to draw the most envy too. Imperfectionists are the ones who are obviously flawed but have the audacity to be active and confident anyway. They make people think, *This person has [XYZ problems] and still has [confidence, fun, success, etc.]. I should have [that], but I'm stuck!*

Back when I was a single perfectionist, I'd see couples and think, *She chose him? I'm in better shape! That guy? I'm better-looking! Him? He seems boring.* I was jealous of everyone who had someone. But I was on the sidelines, not doing anything to find a woman. The reason was, of course, that I feared the imperfect reality of putting myself out there and taking risks. I was stuck.

Then I made a decision to be a single imperfectionist (with the help of the solutions coming in this book). There were two components to it: being content single and accepting imperfect scenarios and conversations with women. I didn't take action perfectly, or even well, but I did it, and it was fun. The first three women I asked out in my new hometown confirmed that this was not going to be a smooth process.

- **Attempt 1:** She had a boyfriend. Trying to be nice, I told her to "have fun with him." *Really, Stephen?*
- **Attempt 2:** She was a lesbian and kissed her girlfriend in front of me.
- **Attempt 3:** I asked her out in a busy gym. She was married.

I'm still single, but I've had more opportunities to meet women and have been on *many* more dates since becoming an imperfectionist. The best part has been the freedom of not needing to be with someone to be content. When you're an imperfectionist, you have fewer limits and can more easily enjoy your imperfect life!

Likability and Trust

If I wanted zero people to like me, I'd say things like this:

My writing is a flawless manifestation of the English language. I'm the best writer in the world.

It's natural to feel put off when someone boasts excessively. But why do you think that is our natural reaction instead of, say, giving them a hug? It's because seeing someone else speak as if they're perfect seems disingenuous and can threaten our egos. It also reminds us of our own imperfection. That said, by the end of this book, I hope you won't mind being reminded of being imperfect.

Now, what if I said the following instead?

I will try my best to communicate a message that adds value to your life. I've put a lot of research and hard work into making this book worth your time.

Compared to the first example, doesn't it decrease your desire to punch me in the face? This version is sincere, honest, and allows room for imperfection. If you act with humility and don't feign perfection, you will be more likable.

I have an interesting question for you. Which one of those introductions would give you greater confidence in the person writing the book? Logically, one might think the self-proclaimed "perfect" writer would write a better book, but most people will tend to believe the exact opposite: *This guy must be a phony!* It's ironic that when we try to appear perfect, the opposite effect is often achieved.

Historically, obvious overcompensation has been associated with dishonesty. You might be familiar with the phrase "snake oil salesman," which has become synonymous with "con artist." And if someone were to try to sell actual snake oil to you today, you'd probably turn them down just because of their association with scams. In truth, Chinese water snake oil contains 20% eicosapentaenoic acid (EPA),[27] which is one of the two kinds of omega-3 fatty acids used by the human body, and it's a higher amount than is found is salmon, which is known for its high EPA (and DHA) content.

Studies have found that omega-3 fatty acids have numerous beneficial health effects.[28] Chinese water snake oil has some value then, but its reputation has been forever tarnished because some snake oil salesmen would overstate its upsides. Snake oil salesmen would often claim it to be a cure-all, and they famously planted "satisfied customers" in the crowd.[29] Others would dilute it or not use actual snake oil. People quickly discredited them (and their snake oil too).

Overcompensation is a psychological indicator of hiding something. It's one more reason for us to scale back on trying to present a perfect image!

Sincerely communicating *effort over perfection* makes us more relatable. Keep this italicized phrase in mind: *effort over perfection*. It's worthy of being a life motto. In fact, it can work as a general solution to perfectionism. When you're wrestling with perfectionism and procrastination, challenge yourself to "try and see what happens."

People trust what they relate to, and they relate to imperfect people doing imperfect things. Have you noticed that the best-received public speakers tend to be humble? Instead of boasting, skilled speakers are far more likely to make a self-deprecating joke. It's smarter to do this if your goal is to connect with people.

Admittedly, it is possible to impress people by boasting, but only if they've first accepted you on an emotional level (otherwise, boasting turns us off). And besides, people are more impressed when you downplay your accomplishments or when someone else boasts on your behalf. This is why it's standard practice for speakers to be introduced by another person who can boast of their accolades. If a speaker walks up and starts his speech by telling the audience how great he is, they might rather leave than hear him speak.

Humility is a psychological indicator in the reverse way of the snake oil salesman: The one who downplays greatness appears even greater. It gives the impression that they've "been there before" and that they don't need to pump themselves up to be and feel worthy.

If you want to be more likable, don't try to appear flawless. Be open about your weaknesses, and don't put up a front. It's really that simple: being imperfect makes people like you more.

The Imperfectionist Process

Imperfectionism is a multistep process. At each stage of the process, it's possible for perfectionism to jump in and ruin things. Here's the complete cycle of a successful, imperfect pursuit:

1. Imperfect thoughts and ideas
2. Imperfect decision
3. Imperfect action
4. Imperfect adaptation
5. Imperfect but successful result

I'll give a real example of mine and point out how perfectionism could have stopped what has been a major blessing in my life at each stage.

1. Imperfect idea: What if I tried starting a blog?

Flaws: barely any blogs make money, I need a job, and it's probably a waste of time.

2. Imperfect decision: Despite my doubts, I'm going to start a blog right now.

Flaws: I don't know where to begin. I have no experience.

3. Imperfect action: I know the first step. I am registering the domain name deepexistence.com. Now I'll figure out how to install WordPress, install a theme, and write and publish posts. Done. Next, I'll write a few guest posts to build traffic. How exciting!

Flaws: it's a time-consuming learning curve, I've already changed themes dozens of times, and my early posts aren't great.

At this point, when you take action, your internal perfectionist gets *much* quieter. This is because the reality of the situation is often 10 times better than a fearful perfectionist projection. You will likely notice flaws as you feared, but it's interesting that once you're in the situation, the flaws won't seem like a big deal.

4. Imperfect adaptation: I created the blog, but it isn't successful. I have just 440 email subscribers after *two years* of hard work, which is well under what many of my peers have done in that time frame. I'm not sure about the design, whether the niche is too broad, and a whole lot more.

Instead of quitting, I'll adapt based on what I've learned. I'll alter my theme yet again, narrow the focus (to the topics of focusing and habit development), increase my writing output, and change my strategy for guest posting.

Flaws: I seem to have failed. It has gone relatively poorly.

5. Imperfect success: Today, I'm living my dream. My blog doesn't directly support me, but it is the platform that I use to launch products, such as books and courses, that do support me financially. Better yet, these products help others live better, which has been the most rewarding facet of my own life.

In the struggle and process of creating a blog that matters, I became a more skilled writer, marketer, researcher, strategist, and editor. I believe this is a key reason why *Mini Habits* has been a best seller ever since its launch. And with these changes, I've attracted over 9,400 subscribers since that slow start.

But it took a while, I thought of quitting *six times,* and you can see how many imperfections there were along the way. At each step of the process, I could have given up because it wasn't perfect. It *still* isn't perfect, but it's good, and I persist!

When you look closely at a human life, this is what it's all about. There is no perfect plan and no perfect scenario, because life happens. As helpful it is to be able to plan, it's equally important to adapt to changing circumstances and problems. It's important to understand that you will be significantly and continually impacted by imperfection—from yourself, the world, and others.

This is the process of an imperfect pursuit. But what about the mindset of an imperfectionist? What does that look like? That's next.

How to Be an Imperfectionist

Up until this point, we've discussed why people are perfectionists, what it does to us, and why we're better off as imperfectionists. I hope that by now you're attracted to the idea of becoming an imperfectionist, because the rest of the book is going to cover how to do that. First, we're going to cover the pivot point of imperfectionism, which can help with *all* subsets.

The reason for starting with a general view and narrowing down to specific solutions is that the problem of perfectionism exists on multiple levels. You can have perfectionism as a general way of thinking, and you can have it in a specific way, such as needing approval or ruminating about past events.

The Lever of Imperfectionism
A lever is "a rigid bar resting on a pivot, used to help move a heavy or firmly fixed load with one end when pressure is applied to the other."[30] It enables you to move something with much less force than if you tried to move the object unassisted. The upcoming insight is like a lever for imperfectionism in that it's easier than a "blunt force" strategy of straight up trying to have more realistic standards. It is the "pivot point" of the imperfectionist mindset.

Pivot point: perfectionism and imperfectionism are determined by what you care about. The following list shows what cares to have (or not) in order to be an imperfectionist. If you follow this advice, I guarantee you'll be happier with your life:

- Care less about results. Care more about putting in the work.
- Care less about problems. Care more about making progress despite them. Or if you must fix something, focus on the solution.
- Care less about what other people think. Care more about who you want to be and what you want to do.
- Care less about doing it right. Care more about doing it at all.
- Care less about failure. Care more about success.
- Care less about timing. Care more about the task.

In general, the idea behind imperfectionism is to not care so much about conditions or results, and care more about what you can do right now to move forward with your identity and your life. Think about this:

People with social anxiety **care more** about social interactions than anyone else does. They care so much about a social interaction going smoothly that they often avoid those situations altogether. And when they're in social situations, they can't act naturally because they're so concerned about how they're coming across, how smoothly and pleasantly the exchange is going, and how something might go wrong.

Depressed people **care more** about shutting down negative thoughts than anyone else does. One day, novelist Leo Tolstoy's brother told him to sit in a corner until he stopped thinking about a white bear. Much later that day,

Tolstoy remained in the corner, his mind fixated on the white bear he needed to stop thinking about. This experiment has been replicated in more studies, and the result is always the same: when people forbid themselves or attempt to rid their mind of something, it boomerangs back to them with alarming consistency and persistency. The solution, then, is to allow negative thoughts but not care about them. In her book, *The Willpower Instinct*, Kelly McGonigal, PhD, says, "Studies show that the more you try to suppress negative thoughts, the more likely you are to become depressed."[31]

Nervous test takers **care more** about their test results than I ever did, and their nervousness may interfere with their ability to recall what they studied.

Speaking of nervousness, after being healthy and calm my whole life, a spider bit me one morning, and a crazy chain of events transpired that sent me to the ER three times and, worse than that, made me begin to unravel mentally. After the spider bite, I overthought every sensation I felt. I started looking for major health problems; from this, I developed a sudden and severe case of general and health anxiety. It got to the point where I'd be visibly shaking in the corner of my bed, worried beyond reason and nervous about my nervousness.

Now I feel as calm as a jellyfish looks, and it's because I finally learned to not care about feeling butterflies in my stomach for no reason. I learned to not care that I was nervous all the time. I acknowledged what was going on, and I didn't care. Apathy saved my skin!

Telling people to stop caring in general is dangerous advice, but if that apathy is in the right place, it can be life-changing in the best way. The right application is the aforementioned list of cares. Here's that list again:

- Care less about results. Care more about putting in the work.
- Care less about problems. Care more about making progress despite them. Or if you must fix something, focus on the solution.
- Care less about what other people think. Care more about who you want to be and what you want to do.
- Care less about doing it right. Care more about doing it at all.
- Care less about failure. Care more about success.
- Care less about timing. Care more about the task.

This is the general direction we're aiming for. It's not only what you care about, it's the intensity as well: Imperfectionism means caring *less* about certain things, because when you care less, you're more relaxed in that area. While relaxed, it means you have no major concerns or distractions, and your mind is clear and primed to focus. This means more mental resources are at your disposal.

Now we'll cover solutions for the five key subsets of perfectionism. If you're worried about keeping track of the solutions, don't. In the final chapter, all proposed solutions will be summarized, "minified" (into actionable mini habits), and placed into a recommended application guide.

Chapter 5

Unrealistic Expectations

"When one's expectations are reduced to zero, one really appreciates everything one does have."

~ Stephen Hawking

Emotions Are Relative to Expectations

Perfectionism and imperfectionism have powerful emotional implications. Perfectionism creates feelings of guilt, anxiety, inferiority, low self-esteem, and irritability. Imperfectionism creates feelings of satisfaction, happiness, joy, calm, and a healthy sense of self-worth.

It's obvious which one sounds better, but who's to say it's accurate? I can *claim* anything, so I'll explain why this is true.

Our emotions are largely derived from our expectations. Generally speaking, when your expectations are met or exceeded, you'll experience a positive emotion, and when they are not met, you'll experience a negative emotion. This is simple and true.

Psychologists Carver and Scheier's cybernetic model of self-regulation states that "emotions emerge from the rate at which behaviors and outcomes meet or fail to meet self-goals."[32] Expectations are essentially weaker versions of self-goals, and the concept applies to them as well. Surprise bonus checks make people smile, and surprise bills upset them.

Perfectionism frequently leads to people being depressed and even suicidal because reality is a disaster in comparison to perfect expectations. Many people try to change their feelings to be more positive in general, but earlier, we discussed how feelings are difficult to change "straight up." For greater optimism, instead of targeting your feelings directly, a more effective strategy is to change what *causes* those feelings.

The most effective strategies for change target the earliest possible part of a process. For example, to eat fewer cookies, it's better to begin with your grocery store shopping rather than relying on willpower when your pantry is already stuffed with cookies. In the same way, **it's best to target your expectations if you wish to change your feelings about something since they're a precursor.**

Expectations are not tangible and inherently meaningful. They're floating meters that tell us how things *should* be. They can be specific or flexible (for example, you could expect to score exactly 18 points or between 15 and 25 points). When reality blows our upper expectations away, we're euphoric. When reality plummets through the floor of our lowest expectation, we're devastated. The level to which we are disappointed or elated is proportional to what we initially expected. Here's a simple example that shows the power of expectations and how they shape our emotions.

At first, money makes people happier, but studies show that this effect decreases with time. This is because with more money comes increased expectations, even for making money itself. If you expect to make $10 working today and you make $100, you'll be overjoyed. But someone who expects to make $1,000 today and only makes $100 will be disappointed. So you can have two people with the exact same result of making $100 who have opposite emotional reactions.

General and Specific Expectations
Okay, it's not *quite* that simple. People have two kinds of expectations—general and specific. If you're looking for the key takeaway now, I'll tell you: **it's best to have high general expectations (for confidence) and low specific expectations (for resilience and confidence).**

General expectations are what you expect from yourself in general. They're your ceiling in life. If you're depressed, so are your general expectations; if you're optimistic and thriving, your general expectations will be high. In the simplest terms, having high general expectations means you're optimistic, but this doesn't apply to any specific scenario or event. Having lower general expectations is a problem not because it forms a ceiling you *can't* surpass but because you *won't try* to surpass it.

We also develop specific expectations for the situations we create and face every day: socializing, working, driving, exercising, and so on. So, for instance, if you're going to a party, you'll have specific expectations about how your social interactions should go. And this is where it gets tricky: perfectionism is a party crasher.

Someone who struggles with perfectionism is more likely to have low general expectations, confidence, and self-esteem *because* they have extremely high specific expectations that are rarely met. For example, their standard for socialization is most likely going to resemble a scene from a James Bond movie because a social perfectionist wants every interaction to be smooth, comfortable, and… well… perfect. Since they rarely (if ever) meet this specific standard, it lowers their confidence and general expectations.

This creates a nasty cycle, because when they enter a conversation (or even before they do), their expectations are shattered instantly. They'll say the wrong thing or say it in the wrong way, or there will be too much silence or not enough, or the topic will be uninteresting, or they'll be sweating, or they'll go into it nervous, or the other person will be nervous, or the eye contact will be awkward, or they'll notice any number of petty human flaws.

That's how having low general expectations and high specific expectations ratchets you into the ground. High specific expectations are unmeetable, which decreases expectations in general, thereby making everything worse. But what if we flipped this scenario around? What if the social perfectionists chose to have high general expectations and low specific expectations?

In this new scenario, the person's general expectations are positive, meaning they have confidence that good things will generally happen in their life. But their specific expectations for socialization are low. By this, I mean they understand that a large number of imperfect happenings are likely to occur in life, and they accept that any given event could go poorly.

Imagine that this person is in conversation and accidentally belches; they say "Excuse me," laugh about it, and carry on. This "terrible happening" lightens the mood even more than usual because it creates an opportunity for people to laugh. When others see that this person is comfortable enough to handle this embarrassing moment, they too become more relaxed. At the end of a night filled with imperfections, this person has had a wonderful time, and their general expectations have increased further. It's not that this person was socially impressive; they just kept their specific expectations in check, never attaching their hopes to any moment, conversation, or even the night itself.

Do you see the difference here? Having low or no expectations for individual events gives you confidence because problems and mistakes won't shock you. When something goes wrong, you'll be relying on your steady, generally high confidence, rather than being like a leaf in the wind, able to be taken off course at the slightest breeze of imperfection.

How ironic is it that the person who expects more from social interactions is the one who contributes and receives less? This is the result of banking on perfection in a flawed world with imperfect people. Placing a perfectionist on planet Earth is like placing potassium in water (it explodes).

Imperfectionism is nothing artificial either. This isn't a "trick" to make you happier. Remember, the unrealistic, ridiculous side of this coin is perfectionism. The idea that we can do anything perfectly is completely and irreversibly contrary to logic, the history of mankind, and every person's experience.

Socializing is just one example of how specific and general expectations can cycle your confidence higher or lower. The same concept applies to getting a job, doing well in an interview, being productive, competing in sports, and countless other activities. When you expect a lot in any specific instance and fall short of it, it damages your confidence and outlook. **If we can create a general confidence in ourselves and stop attaching it to individual happenings, we'll be more consistent winners and will enjoy life more.**

Enough

In 1994, rock star Kurt Cobain of the grunge band Nirvana committed suicide. Cobain wrote a suicide note. In his note were two sentences that suggested he struggled mightily with perfectionism:

"Sometimes I feel as if I should have a punch-in time clock before I walk out on stage. I've tried everything within my power to appreciate it (and I do, God, believe me I do, but it's not enough)."
~ Excerpt from Kurt Cobain's suicide note

Cobain did appreciate performing on stage, but he says that it wasn't enough. After reading much of Cobain's story, I got the sense that he was a severe perfectionist, and his main issue seemed to be unrealistic expectations, and within that, the concept of "enough."

Never Enough

Perfectionists often have a strong "never enough" bias. I want to challenge you to be content in the very moment you read this. Accept your life, as imperfect as it surely is; think *This is enough.*

Contentment isn't passivity. It's the highest-quality setup for personal growth: a mind clear of distractions and a pure no-strings-attached desire to do something that matters to yourself and to the world. Contentment even protects us from feeling stuck and acting passively.

We get stuck when we feel like life is never enough: there's not enough time in the day; we didn't get enough sleep; we didn't do enough this morning; there's not enough money; or we're not good enough for [unlimited reasons].

But the truth is that we can find peace in our limits, our flaws, and the ever-ticking countdown to our deaths. You can be content even in harsh circumstances by focusing on what's right with your life. Are you still breathing? Do you have someone who loves you? Is your cat funny? You can always find something, and you need to find something.

Nobody but you can decide what's enough for you. Many things in society can and do influence our feelings about what is enough, but these feelings are only an influence and not the final decision. Let today be the day that you choose to have enough, and enjoy the freedom and joy that follows.

As for discontentment, it *can* drive positive change. When you're dissatisfied with life, it is often a potent spark for change. So how can you balance the importance of contentment with the "chip on your shoulder" motivation of discontentment?

"Not Quite Enough" Versus "Never Enough"

"Enough" isn't specific enough. It most commonly refers to a sense of satisfaction of quantity (and, to a lesser extent, quality).

Perfectionists with unrealistic expectations struggle with the idea of "never enough." It's discontentment so pure that the motivational boost to change or get more is outweighed by their dissatisfaction with life. It's hopeless, like an addict who always feels the need for one more hit, slot machine pull, drink, cigarette, and so on. This type of "never enough" thinking fuels feelings of distress. No matter how much is done, perfectionists won't allow themselves to feel a sense of contentment and satisfaction.

The positive version of this is called "not quite enough." It means you're not satisfied, but in a healthy way: You haven't had your fill of pull-ups today, you want to write 200 more words of your book, and you're determined to finish your taxes early. This type of "not enough" is healthy ambition to grow as a person!

The difference between these two is that "not quite enough" has an implied end. While "never enough" is like that mechanical rabbit the greyhounds can never catch, "not quite enough" lets us catch the proverbial rabbit; it ends in reward and satisfaction. What interests me is how these two similar phrases have such opposite origins, meanings, and implications.

"Never enough" is rooted in general discontent, malaise, and hopelessness. It implies that satisfaction and contentment are out of reach no matter what one does. Because there is no end in sight, there is no satisfaction—only guilt and shame. **Perfectionists continue to look for satisfaction in what they do when it can only be found in what they think about what they do.**

"Not quite enough" sources from excitement, empowerment, joy, and yes, even contentment. It suggests that a person's needs may already be somewhat satisfied, but they want more, and with more effort, even greater satisfaction can be within reach. When you're thinking "not quite enough," it's not because you feel obligated or guilted into doing more.

If you're a perfectionist, take a close look at these two and learn to identify them in your life. Ask yourself if you're looking at a situation with a "never enough" attitude or a "not quite enough" attitude. The simplest way to identify which one you're using is to identify the emotions that come with it. "Never enough" comes with anxiety, frustration, and hopelessness. "Not quite enough" comes with eagerness, excitement, and hope.

If you fail to establish what *is* enough, you'll inherit the "never enough" mindset. Even if it's an abstract thing, such as writing a quality book, it's possible to set some realistic benchmarks for what you'd like the book to become. This is a skill you can develop with practice, and to do this, simply be mindful of the areas in which you have expectations and then decide what will be enough. Mini habits are a great way to fix this mindset. When you decide that pulling one weed in your garden per day *is* enough, you'll soon find yourself saying it's "not quite enough" and pull a few more.

Forget the Perfect Scenario (Lowering the Bar for Action)

Perfectionists with unrealistic expectations look for perfect scenarios to take action. If they want to write a book, they might only do it when they have a moderate amount of energy, because having low energy is more suitable for watching TV, and having high energy is better for doing something more active. They'll also require themselves to be motivated (i.e., they have to want to do it). They'll only write in their ideal writing spots and on their preferred writing machines. They must have coffee and food! And it must be a full moon.

Those people don't write much.

When this philosophy spreads over one's life like full butter coverage on a piece of toast, it's suffocating. They don't want to settle for nonideal circumstances, but they're missing the point. The point of doing things is simply to do them!

You miss out on too many opportunities when you wait for the perfect scenario to line up, so here's how to change: **Whatever you want to do more of in life—exercise, write, read, swim, dance, sing, laugh, and so on—lower the bar for doing it. If you are willing to do it in the sewer, you will never fail to do it again.**

When I set my exercise bar at one push-up, I started to exercise more frequently, in more situations, and in more places (I've done push-ups in bed, public restrooms, bars, and stores). Over time, this changed my brain's relationship with exercise. Exercise went from a special event to a normal part of everyday life and something I could do anywhere. Because I normalized exercise, I now go to the gym several days a week!

The idea in the last sentence is key. It's life-changing. If something is important to you, it should be your goal to make it casual—not special—because habits are casual. Anything you do habitually is not a special occasion and can even be boring. Think about that in the context of someone who *really* wants to exercise every day. They put it on a proverbial pedestal, and when they get their 30-minute workout done, they feel as if they've done something incredible. At some point, the behavior has to become "normal" to stick, and the secret to getting there is to start there.

Creating your bar for taking action is a choice you fully control. The problem perfectionists face is that they leave their "normal goals" in place, try to change everything else, and then wonder why they can't shake their perfectionism. If you choose to do at least 50 push-ups a day, you're not going to do them in a public restroom. You're not going to do them in your bed. But you could and possibly would do a single push-up in those locations if that's all you had to do. Extrapolate this concept over an entire day, and it gives you *many more* opportunities to make progress.

Setting a low bar for action also switches your focus to the process of lasting change. A high bar requires a great performance. This puts more pressure on you to be perfect, which makes you look for perfect opportunities to perform your perfect task perfectly.

The newfound freedom from setting lower bars for action gives you the all-important sense of autonomy that is inherently lacking in most self-help advice. Over time, you'll realize that you can do more with freedom and confidence than you ever could with high-pressure goals and lofty expectations.

Another way to phrase "unrealistic expectations" is "thinking too much about results." Let's discuss how to focus on the process instead of results, why this is a key focal point of the imperfectionist, and why "result apathy" is the ironic path to incredible results.

Focus on the Process (Result Apathy)

The only way to get results is to go through whatever process leads to them. There's no skipping the process just because you really want something. Imperfectionists ignore results because when you care less about the result of a process, it makes the process itself easier.

Being apathetic about results does NOT mean you're not trying as hard. Not trying comes from *general apathy*. Result apathy is this: "I am going to do my best and not care how it turns out."

This is the golden mindset of life. It might even be… perfect. The common misconception that trips people up is that they don't know *how* to try hard without caring about results; they've never tried it. This is just like the motivation and action connection, where we falsely assume that we need item A to obtain item B. I'm telling you that you can let go of your need for results, perform better, and still get those results!

- **Perfectionists use their desire for positive results to motivate them to go through the process.**
- **Imperfectionists focus on the process and let the results take care of themselves.**

See how imperfectionists are more efficient? They go straight to the process instead of using it as a means to an end. In life, it's always smartest to focus on what you control, and in this case, it's the process, not results. So really, by caring more about the process, it shows you care about the results!

Not only is focusing on results unnecessary to drive effort, but it is also a direct cause or contributing factor of some forms of perfectionism (concern over mistakes, doubts about actions, and rumination). Focusing on the result can provide a weak motivation boost, but it won't make up for distracting us from going through the process.

A List of Results to Stop Caring About
The applications for "result apathy" are numerous:

- Improve your test-taking ability by not caring so much about *your grade*
- Be more relaxed in social situations by not caring so much about *rejection*
- Deliver a better speech by not caring about *mistakes or imperfect delivery*
- Become less anxious by not caring so much about your *anxious thoughts and feelings* (let them be and don't fight them)
- Reduce your depression by caring less about how many *negative thoughts you think*
- Improve your productivity by caring less about *how much (or what quality of) work you get done*

The best way I've found to focus on the process is to have mini habits. By nature, a mini habit is process focused. If you aim for answering one email, that's not an impressive result, but it starts off the process of answering emails and forming this habit. Processes aren't just for results; they help us overcome poor circumstances too.

Responding to Harsh Circumstances

Circumstances are another aspect of unrealistic expectations because you may find yourself in situations you don't expect or feel prepared to face. When circumstances are bleak and you don't know how to handle them, this can cause anything from depression to hopelessness to laziness.

Navy SEALs are more familiar than most with harsh circumstances, and the story of Marcus Luttrell provides an unforgettable lesson in how to handle them. I read Marcus's book, *Lone Survivor*, in two days. I literally couldn't put it down, staying up past 6 A.M. to finish it in one night. It's a riveting story of the brutality and horror of war, but it's also a story of courage containing powerful life lessons. One lesson will never leave me.

People think of Navy SEALs as being very physically fit and skilled in combat. That's true, but it isn't the determining factor for becoming a SEAL. A training officer told Marcus that the grueling SEAL training wasn't a test of physicality but a test of the mind. He explained that the mind is the one to give in first. Marcus recounts a key moment during Hell Week:

"The temperature seemed to grow colder as we jogged around in the freezing surf. And finally they called us out and the whistles blew again. We all dived back onto the sand. Crawling, itching, and burning. Five guys quit instantly and were sent up to the truck. I didn't understand any of that, because we had done this before. It was bad, but not that bad, for chris'sakes. I guess those guys were just thinking ahead, dreading the forthcoming five days of Hell Week, the precise way Captain Maguire had told us not to."[33]
~ Marcus Luttrell, the lone survivor of Operation Red Wings

No matter what you try to do in life, resistance will come. The difficulty will rise to uncomfortable levels. Circumstances and results will be undesirable.

For Marcus, the hardest military training program in the world (Navy Seal BUD/s training) was easy compared to what he'd experience five years later in Afghanistan. Still, his training prepared his mind to focus on the process of surviving in a situation in which so many of us would succumb to dire circumstances.

Most people read a book like this for the story, and I did too, but I also went into it with a strong personal development curiosity: What is it that separates Navy SEALs like Marcus from the rest of us? And what separates men like Marcus even from the elite men who attempt Navy SEAL BUD/s training and quit?

It boils down to thinking about the circumstances or the process. Navy SEALs are mentally special because they keep their mind on the process even in hell-on-earth situations. At their "breaking point," the men who quit during Hell Week were likely thinking ahead as Marcus suggested.

When a circumstantial thinker realizes *I'm tired*, they will loop back to this thought repeatedly, focusing intently on the tiredness. Further actions will be determined by this circumstance—not in a proactive way but in a submissive way. A procedural thinker on a mission who realizes "I'm tired" will snap right back to the process of their mission.

Another way of saying this is that circumstantial thinkers are more drawn to problems than solutions. They're drawn to passive living instead of active pursuance of their goals. The great news is that anyone who currently thinks this way can change.

Winners Focus on the Process
Everything has a process: getting a job, getting in shape, visiting another country, and surviving a battle in Afghanistan when you're outnumbered 35 to one. (It was that lopsided for Marcus's team of four.)

Imagine this: You're with three other soldiers, and more than 100 enemy troops descend upon you from the top of a mountain. Not only do they outnumber you by lethal proportions, but they also have the high ground and are flanking you on both sides. You battle as best you can, but all your comrades are killed around you. You fall back down the rough terrain several times, sustain many painful injuries, and then a rocket-propelled grenade hits the ground next to you, shredding your leg with shrapnel and sending you further down the mountain.

This was Marcus Luttrell's situation. What set him apart in this situation is the same thing that allowed him to complete his training as a SEAL—he focused on the process of survival and kept going back to *What's next?* A SEAL's brutal training teaches them that no matter how hard it gets and how bleak it looks, the best move is to determine and execute the next step.

So many men quit BUD/s training because they stop thinking about what they need to do next and start thinking about how sore and tired they are. Or they imagine the next few days of misery. Circumstantial thinking isn't just focusing on present circumstances; it often takes your mind to the future. Imagine if you were Marcus, badly injured, and you predicted what the next few days would be like based on your current situation. You'd *want* to die.

But Marcus survived. He prioritized his needs and gave himself missions. In his book, he mentions the first mission in the aftermath of the battle that badly injured him and killed his comrades: find water. Being severely dehydrated, his focus on finding water required him to think about the landscape and where water would most likely be. It took his mind off his many problems.

How the Process Can Overcome Poor Circumstances

Nearly all nonideal circumstances have a process that can lead you out of them. For example, imagine your alarm goes off and you know you're supposed to go to the gym this morning, but you're very tired and unmotivated. Here's how the two types of thinkers would react.

The circumstantial thinker: *Why did I plan to work out this morning? I feel exhausted. One more day of rest might be a good idea. My muscles ache. My eyes can barely open, and yet I'm supposed to lift weights today? I don't see how I can do it. I might stay in bed for a few more minutes.* *sleeps for hours*

The procedural thinker: *grunting sounds* *I'll just roll my body off the side of the bed.* *plop* *Ugh! Good. Now I need to walk or crawl to my alarm clock, which is not next to my bed in snooze range.*

The procedural thinker doesn't focus on exercise yet because that's not where the process begins. Difficult processes become easier with "one step at a time" thinking; they are made nearly impossible by looking ahead. It's not that the procedural thinker doesn't hear the circumstantial sob story running through his head. He's just saying, "That's interesting, but I'm still going to start the process and see what happens." Once you're at the gym (or wherever your goal may be) and you get started, you'll be surprised at the inaccuracy of circumstantial excuses.

Focus on the process. It's the single best way to change your circumstances.

Putting It into Perspective

We covered unrealistic expectations in two areas:

- Circumstances are what life's like right now (before action)
- Results are what life could be like (after action)

Ideally, we'll ignore them both. Focusing on either of these hurts our ability to take effective action for the following reasons:

- We might use current *circumstances* as an excuse: I can't run a mile because I'm tired right now.

- We might fear the *results* won't be good enough (another type of excuse): Running will feel miserable, and I won't run long enough for it to matter.

By worrying about our present circumstances or future results, it's *too easy* to justify inaction. For mental freedom, be apathetic about your current circumstances and potential results. Instead, obsess over the process! When you focus on the process, you haven't just lowered expectations, you've bypassed them altogether.

Chapter 6

Rumination

"The tricky thing about rumination is that it feels like it's helpful, but there's no action taken, and you don't move forward to some sort of solution."

~ Carla Grayson

The Beliefs of Ruminators

Rumination is a form of perfectionism in which a person focuses obsessively on their problems and/or the events that caused them. It often involves self-critical thoughts about past performance. Researchers have found rumination to be associated with socially-prescribed perfectionism, which is wanting to be seen in a perfect light by others. Psychologists call it a maladaptive trait—a harmful response to a life challenge.[34]

Ruminators believe (as evidenced by thought or action) the following:

1. Problem solving requires focusing on the problem
2. Others' expectations of them are very high
3. Their identity comes from how well they do (as opposed to what they do and who they are)
4. Negative chance outcomes are personal failures
5. Time travel exists (I'm only half-joking, as excessive analysis of the past suggests a desire to change it)

Undoing the rumination habit requires unraveling the beliefs that create it. We'll cover how to conquer rumination by accepting sunken costs, understanding chance versus failure, focusing on the present, correcting poor self-talk, and taking action in your area of rumination.

Acceptance into Action

In 1985, Nintendo released a video game called *Super Mario Bros.* It spawned several series and spinoffs, and the iconic character's games have netted hundreds of millions of dollars, making Mario the highest-paid plumber ever. Most people know of this first game: it's a platformer game in which the player is tasked with moving left to right and jumping over obstacles and onto enemies' heads in order to progress through levels.

For most levels of *Super Mario Bros.*, you go at your own pace, and they allow you to travel backward if you wish, but a select few levels automatically scroll forward, and if you don't actively move with the camera, the edge of the screen will push you off a ledge or crush your body against a pipe. Life is like this second style of auto scrolling, in that if you don't continue to move forward (like if you're ruminating about the past), you're going to face trouble.

There are two types of things we ruminate about—fixable and non-fixable things.

Non-fixable Rumination? Acceptance Is Imperative

A sunken cost is some kind of irreversible damage, cost, or misfortune. The only healthy response to a sunken cost—no matter how devastating it may be —is to accept it. You know you've accepted a sunken cost when you're no longer wishing it didn't happen.

I tried advertising on a blog for my *Mini Habit Mastery* video course and only regained $50 in sales of the $250 I invested in it. That was a sunken cost (but it's tax deductible... yay!).

It's relatively easy to not ruminate about losing advertising money. But the event of rumination may be tragic; the tragedy may even be your fault. At some point, we must realize that no amount of guilt, remorse, and rumination can change what has already happened. Time doesn't stop and go backward, and neither should we, or else our thorny past will wrap us in its painful grasp and cause damage beyond the initial event.

It's *never* disrespectful (to those you've hurt) to move on with your life, as rumination doesn't solve problems or make up for mistakes. Self-punishment doesn't atone for things you've done or make the situation better. **Rumination is a desperate, futile attempt to change the past by thinking about it. It's a form of denial, and acceptance is the antidote.**

Acceptance means that you'll be hit with the full force of the pain—and it will hurt if it's something serious—but once you do it, you give yourself the best chance to move beyond it. Acceptance of *your humanity* is equally paramount. You're allowed to make mistakes—even horrific ones—because you're human.

We each have a personal line regarding what we think is acceptable as a mistake. We'll allow ourselves to break a glass once in a while, but what about accidentally running over a pedestrian with a car? That's an extreme example that very few of us will experience, but it's something that can happen to anyone who drives. It's something that I assume is beyond the line of an "acceptable mistake" for most of us. At this point, the choice is to try to live with an unforgivable mistake or to forgive yourself. Forgiveness is the better choice, but how is this done?

If you've made a mistake that's beyond your acceptable line, you must move the line.

There is no benefit in drawing the line *before* the worst thing you've done. In other words, no matter what you've done, you have to give yourself a break or your mind will break trying to reconcile your mistake with your lack of tolerance for it. (It's like a computer trying to divide by zero: your mind won't understand how to solve the problem.)

After you accept what is, you're free to look for what could be. Of course, it's easier said than done to "just accept what's happened." You may have to live it before you feel it. Some things will take longer than others to get over, but I believe the process can be sped up by creating a purposeful daily reminder that the past is not changeable.

Fixable Rumination? Accept It and Try Again

If you crash your motorcycle but know someone who can fix it (and your broken arm), then it's only a matter of time and money before you can literally get back to full speed. If you submit a proposal to your boss and she says, "That's the worst project proposal I've ever seen," you can listen to her advice and submit another one later. **Almost all things people ruminate about are solvable problems.**

Conceptual example: I'm ruminating about how I should have written this sentence better. Well, hey, instead of doing that, I could go ahead and write this next sentence, which takes my mind off of the poor first sentence and brings my attention to writing this also-poor second sentence. I can continue this chain until I write a sentence that I accept; in doing this, I'm making the present moment productive rather than fixating on my poorly written past.

We have the amazing power of choice, and rumination is giving up that power. It's a destructive, but easy, habit to form. The fix is to continue to try, practice, and improve, and in time, you'll see how ridiculous it is to ever ruminate about something that you can fix or try again.

The core solution for rumination is taking action to get your mind to a better place. If it's unfixable, pursue your interests. If it's fixable, take action in the exact area you're tempted to ruminate on. But how can one develop the persistence necessary to keep trying despite mistakes and failures? The answer is next, and it's exciting for anyone who easily gets discouraged by failure.

Understanding Chance Versus Failure

A slight shift in mindset in regard to your concept of failure can change your life. It has changed mine. Ruminators—and people in general—often mislabel chance as failure, but if you can draw a line between chance and failure, you will instantly ruminate *much* less often.

In a nutshell, chance outcomes cannot be considered failures. One might call a chance result "failure" in the strictly technical sense of the word (i.e., not a successful result), and that's fine. Most of us, however, think of failure as a performance-based mistake or shortcoming of our own doing. This definition of failure carries far more implications than a technical "that didn't work" definition. Since chance-based outcomes aren't up to us, we can't apply that definition of failure to them.

The Statistics of Failure
Nobel Prize winner and psychologist Daniel Kahneman was confused. After conducting several interrelated studies, the results were contradictory. He analyzed the data from every angle, but he couldn't make sense of the information.

Finally, he realized his error; Kahneman had selected sample sizes that were too small to give reliable results.[35] Though he is well versed in statistics, he still chose sample sizes based on tradition and his intuition (rather than on statistical principles). He wondered if this could be a widespread occurrence, so he put two other prominent statisticians, who had authored a statistics textbook together, to the test.

They made the same mistake.

We make this mistake too. We often fail to consider instances of failure in the context of statistics.

Imagine: A man walks up to a stranger and asks him for directions. The man brushes him aside and ignores his question. Ouch. In the next week, two more people do the same. He's been rejected three times now. How does he interpret this?

Either strangers aren't friendly, or people don't like me, he thinks. HALT, SIR! I have to pull the statistics card here. He interacted with three people. There are seven billion people on Earth. Statistically speaking, even the friendliest person in the friendliest city would be susceptible to a triple brush-off. If he presented his conclusion to a statistician, here's how he might respond:

"Wait, wait. Oh, this is good." *snickering* "You're saying that from a population of seven billion, you've made a firm conclusion based on a sample size of THREE? Haaaa! What was the standard deviation on that one? Bwaaaahahaha! Oh, tell me another one!"
~ Statistician with a sick, statistics-based sense of humor

The Difference between Chance and Failure

Talking to a stranger is chance based. They might be busy, disinterested, friendly, or any other disposition. Applying for a job? Chance. Asking anyone for anything? Chance. The results can be affected by our behavior and choices, but they are still outside of our control.

This explains why persistence is chance's best friend, because if you continue to try a chance-based venture, you will probably succeed in time.

What would a statistician tell a wanna-be-published writer to do? Submit your manuscript everywhere, and be aggressive about it. Sure, if it's terrible, you won't get anywhere (unless there are vampires in it). But if it's decent or even masterful, the more you send it out, the better your chances of getting an offer. The fastest-selling books in history are the last four *Harry Potter* books, but the first of the series was rejected 12 times before it was published. As the success of the *Harry Potter* books have proven, author J. K. Rowling is not the one who failed those 12 times.

The same applies to every chance-based pursuit. This means that if something unfortunate happens, but it was chance-related, you have no *right* (let alone reason) to feel like you personally failed. This should come as an instant relief to all of us who have been turned down for jobs, dates, opportunities, and awards. When other people are deciding who wins, who gets a raise, or who gets a book published, it's chance. This perspective puts disappointing chance-based results behind you immediately. (You will have to remind yourself often of this in the beginning.)

Failure is different, and it's highly useful to us.

- Failure is what Thomas Edison encountered numerous times before he found the successful formula for the lightbulb.
- Failure is trying to pursue a goal that's bigger than your current

willpower capacity.

- Failure is touching a hot stove with your hand and getting burned.

Unlike chance, failure is a fully predictable result. Failure is really nice. I mean it. It's even more comforting than chance because it's easier to interpret. What if you touched 10 various surfaces and didn't know which one burned you? You might be afraid to touch vinyl if that were the case. You know it's failure when it doesn't work well in any circumstance.

There can be some overlap between chance and failure, because if you take a chance with the wrong strategy, you'll *probably* fail each time. In many cases, it's hard to know; so if a person turns you down for something, ask why. It takes courage to ask for feedback when you've been turned down, but it can be invaluable to help you see what you could do differently next time.

Sometimes, people email me asking me for a favor when I've never met them. Like many people who receive lots of emails, it's an instant "no" answer that often gets no response. But if they were to send me an email asking me why I didn't respond or what they could do to tweak their approach, I'd tell them. People are usually willing to give you honest feedback when you ask for it.

Here are the takeaways. Let these sink in for a better life:

- **If something is chance based, be stubbornly persistent.** There's no reason to quit a (free) chance-based venture. Ever. It's irrational to quit unless it costs you something. It's free to submit guest post articles, ask women to go to dinner with you, apply for dream jobs, or ask your boss for a raise. There can be many upsides if you get positive results, so take action without apologizing. Be the most aggressive person you know!
- **If something fails, try a different approach.** Concrete failure, as opposed to chance failure, gives you an opportunity to eliminate that way of doing things (Edison's failed lightbulb prototypes are a popular example of this).
- **When you suspect a negative result comes from a combination of chance and failure, be persistent, but try varying strategies to the degree that you think it's failure.**

I once submitted a guest post to the popular blog MindBodyGreen. I worked hard on it and thought it was a great post, but they didn't even tell me "no." I didn't hear from them. I sent another one. No response. I sent a third one, which was the best post yet. They ignored me again.

Others continued to write for them, so I decided that this was likely a case of concrete failure. Because I had no feedback, I asked a friend who had posted for them, and I took his advice. Instead of writing about what I thought was important, I studied their most popular articles in greater depth, picked a relevant topic that hadn't been covered, and wrote a post about that. Bingo! My fourth submitted guest post was accepted. I've since written several times for them.

Understanding chance and failure is the key to getting what you want out of life. It protects you from the sting of rejection, implores you to persist, and enables you to adapt to life like a pro.

Take on this new perspective, and rumination about your performance isn't likely to happen. You might feel bad about a poor result, but rumination is only a problem when it *lingers*, and it's unlikely to linger when you have a clear next step of trying again with or without a new strategy.

"Should" and Self-Talk

The language we use has a lot to do with how often and to what extent we ruminate, and it's one of the easiest "fixes" we can employ to thwart rumination.

"Should" is a dangerous word because when used in reference to the past ("should have"), it implies that something was done incorrectly and should have been done differently. It suggests some amount of regret.

"Should have" is a phrase of suggestion, and it comes fully loaded with guilt and shame. Ruminators commonly think about what they *should have* done differently when looking back on an event or sequence of events, often ignoring the positive things they did.

That said, there's no need to get carried away if you happen to say, "I should have ordered cream cheese with this bagel." That's an innocent version of "should have" that has no need for correction. Besides, cream cheese is delicious. The context and tone of your self-talk reveals a lot about your self-relationship.

While I was visiting Hawaii, I walked up to a homeless man. He was sitting against a brick wall and looked to be in need of something. I asked if I could get him some food from the grocery store nearby. He asked for cigarettes. I almost got them for him, as I wanted to make his night, but not in that way. So I asked him if there was anything else I could get him from the grocery store, and after pressing for a cigarette alternative, he said he'd drink Mountain Dew (a lesser evil).

I brought him back soda and some chocolate. But when he realized I hadn't bought him cigarettes, he furrowed his brow and said emphatically, "I'm so stupid! I'm such an idiot!" Supposedly, he was upset with himself that he hadn't been able to convince me to buy him cigarettes. He despised himself.

It's odd to think that we have a relationship with *ourselves*, but it's true and especially clear when you look at the flat-out abusive relationship that man had with himself. When ruminating, you're judging yourself for what you did just as you would another person. Even though you're the same one who took the action, your analytical side can act as if it's a different (and highly critical) person when you're ruminating. Ruminators can learn to relate to themselves in a friendlier way, and this starts with improving self-talk.

How Can You Change Poor Self-Talk?

1. Seek to understand.

Poor self-talk can be addressed with the same communication techniques used to improve unhealthy relationships (since this is a "self-relationship"). In his book *The 7 Habits of Highly Effective People*, author Stephen Covey says to "seek first to understand, then to be understood." This is great advice for relationships and for your inner ruminator.

Action: When you begin to ruminate on an event, give yourself 30 seconds to understand why you did what you did. You always act in your perceived best interest. Think about your motives in that moment. Admit you're a flawed person. Once you've fully understood your "prior self" in that moment, you will not judge your actions as harshly (just as the key to judging other people less is to try to understand them more). We're hardest on ourselves when we don't take a moment to understand.

People who are addicted to harmful substances can be really hard on themselves for giving in, but if they took a moment to understand the nature of addiction and the difficulty of being human, they'd have more compassion on themselves and feel less guilty, which could help to pull them out of the common guilt-addiction cycle.

2. Say "could" instead of "should."

If you cut your finger off with a table saw, you might think about how you should have been more careful or used proper safety equipment. I think that's a useful thing to learn. The real problem with rumination, then, is time. It's healthy to consider how alternate decisions may have affected outcomes, but when it is obsessive and beyond what's necessary, the benefit quickly gets overshadowed by wasted time and recycled negative thoughts.

The language we use has a lot to do with how much time we spend thinking about the past.

A great substitute for "should have ___" is "could have ___." This is the phrase of possibility. Whereas "should" evokes a sense of certainty and obligation, "could" is open-ended and free. This open-ended perspective of life makes more sense, because our life paths are not always what they first seem.

- I should have danced more = shame on me for not dancing more
- I could have danced more = I recognize I could have danced more

If I had to choose my single greatest regret, I'd say it was going to college, just because it wasn't very useful for me personally. But going to college is the very path that brought me to where I am today, where I'm happy to be. That's why I don't regret it. That's why I can't say for certain that I "should not have gone to college."

It's better to use the open-ended "could have" because it's impossible to calculate the total present and future impact of the decisions we make and the things that happen to us. Saying you certainly should or shouldn't have done something is terribly shortsighted.

I made mistakes in interviews that likely contributed to me not finding a job after college. But missing out on those opportunities pushed me to work hard to create my own career path. At the time, I may have said, "I shouldn't have said that." But if I got a job immediately after graduating—which was the plan—I doubt I'd have written a book that's being published in more than a dozen languages right now.

Make a mental note to flag anytime you think of what you "should" have done. When you catch yourself doing this, reevaluate the situation and replace it with "could."

Be Active in the Present Moment

In the acceptance part of this chapter, we talked about why taking action is an important step. This section will give you specific strategies for doing this.

Ruminators' big problem is not getting back out there:

- The man who bombs the interview focuses on what he should have said instead of moving on and applying for more jobs (or even contacting the company again).
- The woman who says the wrong thing at dinner avoids talking further, goes into her shell, and ruminates on how she should not have said that, rather than making up for it.
- The man who stays silent instead of asking the pretty woman to dinner ruminates on his failure to act as he misses the next opportunity to do so (and then he'll ruminate on that).
- The woman who injures herself at the gym dwells on her misfortune instead of immediately setting up a doctor's appointment to get back into form.
- The boy ruminates on a poor test grade he received, rather than studying for the next one.

If you ruminate on the small things, you will ruminate about the big things because that's how you've trained yourself to handle negative happenings. Rumination can become a habitual response that gets worse over time; when it gets bad, people will ruminate about things that happened weeks, months, or even years ago.

We've already covered some of the solutions to rumination: accepting the past as unchangeable, understanding the not-so-intimidating nature of chance and failure, and creating healthy self-talk. This puts us in a prime position for the next step of the process. And this is a process—not a quick flip of a switch.

If you find yourself ruminating about something, come back and go through this process. As you move through it, the subsequent steps become easier. For example, it may be extremely difficult to focus on the present moment right away when you catch yourself ruminating, but if you first accept the past, consider chance and failure, and adjust your self-talk, it will become much easier.

Once you've detached yourself somewhat from your object of rumination using the prior techniques, it's time to take action. My favorite tools to use for impromptu action are timer-based action prompts.

How to Be Active Using Timers

Timers can give you a cue to take action, add gentle pressure to encourage you forward, and create a structure for work and reward. The following techniques have worked well for me.

The Countdown Starter: When the timer runs out, you must start your task immediately.

When you need to get started on a task, but motivation is low and you're stalling, run a countdown timer. This works every time for me. To combine it with the mini habits strategy, pinpoint the first very small action you can take to move forward. For example, if you're resisting exercise, you can change into gym clothes (or, more specifically, put on gym shorts). Commit to taking that first step when the timer hits zero.

The reason this works is because it gives us a clear starting point. When you can start "anytime," you'll often choose to procrastinate. As for how long to give yourself, this may vary with context. When I use this method and I'm not busy with something else, I often give myself 60 seconds—just enough time to relax and prepare myself for taking action.

The Decision Countdown: You must make a firm decision before the timer runs out!

Use a countdown timer to put gentle pressure on yourself to make a specific decision or a general "I need to do something, but what?" decision. Putting this pressure on yourself and practicing it daily is a great way to improve your decision-making confidence and speed. Pressure is a little bit uncomfortable, but as long as it isn't overbearing, it is very useful to get us moving!

Make sure you give yourself enough time to deliberate over your options— but not too much time. I've found the sweet spot for me to be three- to 10-minute countdowns, depending on the complexity of the decision.

The Focus Timer: For X minutes, you must focus on one task of choice (with strict rules for distractions).

When I do this, I often exceed my target time because I'll become absorbed in the task.

Tip: If you have a Mac, use the full-screen function, which completely blocks out everything but that one program. Set a rule that you can't switch to another program for any reason until time runs out. Trust me, even little things like, "I think I'll check my email" are deceptively lethal to productivity. Small concessions spawn distraction just as small forward steps generate productivity. Don't move away from your focus area for any reason.

If it seems too hard to focus completely on one thing for very long, you simply need practice. Set your goal for five minutes of focus and work your way up to a more substantial amount of time. What you practice on a daily basis—whether it's distracting yourself or focusing—is what you'll "get good at." Most people today are adept at responding to text and Facebook notifications and not very skilled at focusing on important things. With practice, we can change that!

The Pomodoro Technique: Work 25 minutes, rest five minutes. Repeat.

This is a popular technique that works well. My only gripe is that when I'm focused on a project, I will work for more than minutes. I'm not convinced that 25 minutes is magical or that it should be the same amount of time each day. I go more by feel. Sometimes, I know I can focus for an hour or more. At other times, I'm lucky to get 20 minutes (or so I think until I get started!).

That said, the principle is sound, it will work, and it is much better than nothing. From the Pomodoro website, here is the Pomodoro process[36]:

1. Decide on the task to be done
2. Set the timer to 25 minutes
3. Work on the task until the timer rings
4. Put a checkmark on paper to signify completion
5. Take a short break (three to five minutes)
6. Every four "pomodoros," take a longer break (15–30 minutes)

The Work and Play Carousel: Work for an hour, relax for an hour. Repeat.

This back-and-forth technique rewards you handsomely for each segment of work you do.

"But that break is way too long!"
~ Randomly Selected Reader

If you think it's a bad idea to increase your relaxation time, consider this: Greeks worked an average of 2,034 hours in 2012, while Germans worked an average of just 1,397 hours.[37] And while Greeks worked more hours, Germans were 70% more efficient in terms of GDP per hour worked (making them more productive overall despite working 600+ fewer hours per person!). It's not a perfect comparison because of other socioeconomic factors in these countries, but it drives home the point. **Time spent working is an incomplete measure of productivity**.

An hour of hard, focused work can absolutely be worth two hours of reward in some cases. You've likely had times when you "worked" for four hours and accomplished very little and times when you worked for 20 minutes and deserved a trophy for all you accomplished.

Parkinson's Law states that work contracts or expands to fill the time you allot for it. If you give yourself more time for relaxation and less time for work, you might find yourself doing more to maximize your work efficiency because of this phenomenon. One more thing: consider the increased energy you'll have from being well rested, which can be utilized for better focus and higher work intensity.

Should you use this or the Pomodoro technique? Try both. The Pomodoro technique is based on giving your body and brain short breaks for rest and revitalization purposes (to help you prepare for another session of work). This "carousel" technique is based more on creating a better reward. In theory, this could generate a higher positive neurological association between work and play. The brain always prefers the activities that directly precede rewards (as we know from the science of habit structure).

Timer Tools

I recommend you try all these techniques and see which one works best for you. Now that you have the methods, you need a timer! Here are some free timer tools you can use:

- Simple kitchen timer (an actual physical, not-digital timer device!): A physical kitchen timer is hard to beat because you can start a physical timer faster than you can an app timer.
- Digital kitchen timer (Android): Yes, there's an app for that. This app even has three independent timers you can activate. I'm not sure why you'd want three, but the option is there.

- Alarm Clock Xtreme Free (Android): This is what I use. It's my alarm clock, but the app also has a tab for setting a countdown timer.
- Timer Tab (http://timer-tab.com): This is a good one if you work online, because as the name indicates, the time left can be seen in your browser tab.
- iPhone and iPad: No apps needed! The iOS operating system has a timer app built into it. Select the clock app and you'll find "timer" as one of the tabs. Set your time and click start, and you can select which ringtone to use when the time runs out.

Rumination Quick Guide

For reference, here is a recap of how to overcome rumination. There will also be a summary in the last chapter.

Rumination is a focusing problem—you're looking into the past with regret (or hope for a time machine) instead of looking at what you can do now to live your best life. Whenever you catch yourself ruminating on anything negative about your past, here's what you can do to turn it around:

1. Accept the past as unchangeable. At your selected daily cue (time, location, or following another habitual activity), take a moment to reflect on and accept the finality of the past. This is good practice to develop a "present mindset."

2. If it's performance-related rumination, identify it as chance or failure. If chance, try again. If failure, celebrate that you've ruled out one method and think of something else to try. If you suspect it's a combination of both, such as when you're rejected repeatedly, continue to try again with new strategies.

3. Monitor your self-talk. If you find yourself thinking in terms of "should have," rephrase it to "could have" to evoke a sense of possibility instead of judgment. Also seek to understand your decision-making in that moment. We generally have reasons for everything we do, so try to understand your reasoning at the time as if you are having to defend your prior self in court.

4. Be active. Rumination's big problem is inactivity. It's not possible to focus effectively on something in the present if your mind is in the past. To help spark yourself to activity, be sure to have daily mini habits, but also use the mini habit philosophy of "sparking" action in any area by starting extremely

small and using timers. For example, if you're ruminating about an argument you had, make it your goal to dial a friend and hit "send." Before long, you'll be laughing about something else, or you'll be able to navigate through your emotions with your friend's help.

EXAMPLE:

Jerry made it to the second round of a job interview, but he's ruminating about it because they chose someone else. He's thinking about how he should have said things differently, and is disappointed that he was turned down for the job. His fist is clenched in frustration. While he realizes that ruminating on it isn't useful, he's having a tough time letting go, so he goes through the steps outlined in this chapter.

1. Jerry reflects on the finality of not getting the job. Since they hired someone else, he realizes that even persistence wouldn't work in this case. Understanding that the job is completely out of his reach helps him to begin to detach from it emotionally.

2. Jerry realizes that this job was a chance-based pursuit, and that his performance actually was good enough to get the job. When he was ruminating on what he said before, it was mainly because he tried to make sense of why he didn't get hired. Now that he has accepted the negative result in step one and released his emotional attachment to getting the job, he sees the situation more objectively. From this conclusion, Jerry is already thinking about where he'll apply to next.

3. Earlier, Jerry was thinking about what he "should have" said. He reframes that to what he "could have" said, which is not only less judgmental and stressful, but will also help him in future interviews. He writes down a few notes on how he might improve for his next interview, and feels better that his experience taught him something.

4. Jerry is already applying for another job, and now that he's focused on new opportunities, he's completely moved on from the disappointing result of this last job. He sees it as a waste of time to think on it further. He's no longer ruminating!

Chapter 7

Need for Approval

"People who want the most approval get the least and people who need approval the least get the most."

~ Wayne Dyer

Why Do People Seek Approval?

People seek approval for two main reasons:

1. They lack self-confidence and self-esteem, and thus look for other people to give it to them. People who lack confidence tend to seek permission for their actions. This means that they value others' opinions more than their own. Remember, it's not self-confidence when someone else gives it to you!

2. They want to be liked by everyone. When a person feels the need to be liked by everyone, it affects all of their actions. It can get so pervasive that it impacts their behavior even when they're alone, because they'll imagine people or a certain someone watching their every move. The solution for this is something I call rebellion practice, which is as fun as it sounds.

Your Confidence Will Soar as an Imperfectionist

Low confidence means uncertainty, and when you're uncertain about something, you'll seek further validation. One solution to the problem of needing approval, then, is to increase your self-confidence. With high self-confidence, you don't need approval to feel validated and worthy.

The following confidence-building solutions are effective because they're practice-based. You can't transform your confidence by thinking about it. You have to build it through experience and action.

The Three-Pronged Confidence Approach

1. Chemical Confidence Building

Earlier in the book, I mentioned Cuddy's study, which found that, after standing in a confident pose for two minutes, participants' testosterone increased by 20% and their cortisol decreased by 25%. Those are significant confidence-boosting chemical changes for just two minutes of easy "work."

It's hard to think of a situation where this *couldn't* be used, as confidence is such an integral part of all aspects of life.

Given the results of this study, it's not crazy to suggest confidence pose training for those with low self-esteem. This is a temporary solution, but, if practiced daily, it could become more permanent through practice. And it's easy to practice: just open up your wingspan!

Confident poses are marked by taking up more space: a wide stance, open chest, and upright posture. Submissive poses—which were found to have the opposite (negative) effect of increasing cortisol and lowering testosterone—are marked by making yourself smaller: curling up in a ball, crossing your arms or legs, and slouching.

Walking around in public like you're a bird in flight might not be the answer. For more low-key training, you can use this trick situationally, like holding a confident pose in the bathroom before an interview (they tested this specific example and it worked well). Or how about a confident pose before a date, presentation, or meeting? Any pose where you open up your chest and take up space should work.

2. Faking Confidence

I'm a proponent of "fake it 'til you make it." The strategy sounds bad because nobody wants to be fake. But all it means is suspending your self-doubt for a moment to allow yourself to think and act like a confident person. If you have never acted confident before, you need to *practice* doing it, and it won't feel sincere at first.

If you have an opportunity to fake confidence when you don't feel it, by all means practice. It is no different than your mindset for acting in a play or movie. Create a confident persona in your mind, pretend you're that person, and then act it out.

Some people may find it to be insincere or even too difficult to act against strong feelings of self-doubt. There's a way to practice being confident without needing to "fake it," and that's adjusting your benchmark.

3. Adjusting Your Benchmark

The traditional way to boost confidence is flawed because it *only* focuses on boosting the self. The two solutions above can work to do that, but boosting yourself is only half of the equation, because confidence is *always* relative to something. **Confidence does not actually exist as a standalone attribute.** Even general confidence is a function of how competent you believe you *generally* are compared to whatever standard you have in your mind.

Why else would your confidence fluctuate? After being turned down for 10 jobs, you might have lower confidence, and that's because you suddenly see yourself as below the benchmark, not because you have changed! As self-focused beings, we tend to take too much credit for things when in fact we're more predictable than our environment is.

Most people focus on their confidence internally and don't see the relativity. This is why people will only and always suggest that you try tactics to "boost your confidence" and "believe in yourself." There's nothing inherently wrong with this advice, but, since confidence is relative, we must also consider what it is relative to!

Imperfectionists are the most confident people in the world, and it's not because they're intrinsically superior. Imperfectionists are masters of customizing their benchmark to fit *them*. They actively decide what they're going to be confident about. To give you an example of relative confidence, think about these five scenarios and your confidence of having success in them:

1.   Racing a giant tortoise (max speed = 0.2 MPH)
2.   Racing a chicken (9 MPH)
3.   Racing your neighbor (that's Betsy, and she runs at 13 MPH)
4.   Racing the world's fastest man, Usain Bolt (27.78 MPH)
5.   Racing a cheetah (70 MPH)

These all relate to one thing—how fast you are. But the answer to that question changes with each move down the list. Did you feel your confidence gradually shriveling as you moved toward the cheetah? That's how relative confidence works. Against a giant tortoise, we're all speed demons! Against a cheetah, even Usain "The Human Lightning" Bolt will get embarrassed. Your confidence in your foot speed depends on what relative benchmarks you consider to be adequate, poor, or remarkable.

If you're not confident in an area or in general, ask yourself, "Where is my benchmark set?"

I'm confident in my running speed, but that's only because my benchmark isn't a cheetah or Usain Bolt! In fact, I remember one time in high school I participated in a casual race. At the time, I thought I was probably the second fastest man alive (seriously), but I was shocked when a couple of the guys shot off the line like rockets well ahead of me. Me! I felt like a slug because those guys raised my benchmark so high. I regained my confidence later, when I once again seemed really fast compared to the people around me. I didn't get faster. My benchmark got more realistic.

These benchmarks exist in every area: attractiveness, intelligence, social skills, strength, humor, and confidence itself (how confident you are in your confidence level). We're continually calculating our competency in different areas against our fluctuating benchmarks.

I suspect that many of us use the "average person" model to determine our confidence. We have an idea of what the average person is like in an area and judge ourselves based on that concept. But this is a deeply flawed way to handle confidence. It's like buying an "average shirt" instead of buying your size. It might (and does) work for some people, but it's not going to work for most of us.

The "average" in an area is not authoritatively significant, and would be hard to nail down anyway, given the conceptual, non-concrete, subjective nature of most of these areas. You might think you're average-looking at best, but to one person, you might be the most attractive person. You might think you're really funny, but compared to Jim Carrey, I think we're all pretty boring.

People will still derive their confidence from silly benchmarks: what they think is normal, what the people in their life are like, or what they see on TV. **Every confidence benchmark is arbitrary, so we may as well create our own.**

One of the keys to my transformation into an imperfectionist has been customizing my confidence. The only stable confidence is what you define and customize for yourself. Otherwise, it will fluctuate dramatically based on the information you receive from others (which adjusts your floating benchmark). We've got to take control of our benchmarks.

Confidence Customization

The right perspective of confidence is not to *assess* your confidence level and pump yourself up to where you want to be. If you aren't confident that you can deliver a killer speech, no amount of psyching up is going to change that. Only practice can gradually change that. So what can you do in the meantime? Be confident that you can deliver a lousy or average speech.

The key to building powerful confidence is to decide specifically what you can be confident about right now, and build from there.

When people aren't confident in themselves about something, they tend to fight it emotionally instead of strategically. But remember: the theme of this book is strategy over emotional manipulation. Rather than working on yourself, work on your benchmark, because it's easier to change.

Let me give you a personal example. One of the worst areas of perfectionism for me was romance, as you may have gathered from earlier examples. My benchmark for suaveness and confidence was James Bond. This all but made me unable to approach women I was interested in. It crushed my confidence because I'm not James Bond (but ladies, I'm pretty close … ish). Instead of trying to build myself up to believe I was 007, which hadn't worked in the past, I changed my benchmark. I waved my imperfectionist wand and turned my benchmark into a giant tortoise. I am slightly more suave (and much faster) than a giant tortoise.

My new benchmark in practical terms was to say "Hi" to women. That was something I decided I was confident I could do, and I did it! There was no pressure to make them laugh or swoon. A couple months later, I was asking out strangers, one of whom said I had "balls of steel" and that I "must be really confident" to approach her on the Stairmaster in front of a couple dozen people at the gym. You can see there was rapid progression in my confidence, but why do you think this works?

Consider what a benchmark means. If James Bond is your benchmark for suaveness with women, that's insanely high, but it's also *enough*. You're not going to reach James Bond status and then be insecure because you're not the 2.0 version of Bond. No. Bond level is enough. And for me, I made saying "Hi" enough. "Enough" is one of the most anti-perfectionist concepts in the world.

When you set a benchmark you can confidently reach every time, you can't care what happens after you meet it. That's an obvious truth if your benchmarks are sky high, but when you set them low, it must be said that you cannot treat yourself like the greyhound chasing that pesky rabbit around. Allow yourself the feeling of success for meeting your benchmark, because you're creating a foundation for confidence.

The bonus effect of this is that you'll be more likely to overachieve after you meet that benchmark. If you feel successful, then you'll naturally relax and stop worrying about "measuring up," which is exactly how confident people act! So really, this works in two ways.

The two factors at play are ability and confidence. First, you must be able to do something. Then you can do it confidently. When I first began this "Hi" benchmark, I didn't always *say* it confidently. I was only confident in my *ability* to *do* it, not in my ability to do it confidently. Before, I was unable to be like James Bond, and so I rarely tried, rarely practiced, and had no chance of developing real confidence. The benchmark isn't so that you can automatically appear confident—that will come in time, possibly sooner rather than later—it's to ensure you get your practice in.

Doing something with confidence requires practice because confidence is comfort. If you're confident in your carpentry skills, you're comfortable with your carpentry skills. If you're confident in general, you're comfortable with yourself in most situations.

Confident people don't need approval or validation from others, because they have both within themselves. Confidence is a skill you can practice and improve.

Permission and Embarrassment

Needing approval creates a wall between you and your ideas.

Like all forms of perfectionism, needing permission threatens our freedom. You might begin to see decisions made without external validation as being too risky, simply because validation adds that extra layer of comfort and security (kind of like your doctor telling you it's okay to do something).

Maybe it's because of how we're raised as children, or maybe it's insecurity, but a great number of us are far too reliant on permission to act. Permission is a big part of our external lives—there are rules all around us (a rule is a requirement or a lack of permission to do something). We have federal laws and state laws, company policies, social norms and etiquette, and so on.

Some rules are necessary to keep things orderly, but often it can get to the point where we fear we're breaking some kind of rule for things that don't matter. Is it okay to eat ice cream at 3 PM? Is it socially acceptable to walk up to a stranger and start a conversation? Is sending four emails in a row to the same person within reason? Even if the answer is no, those rules can be safely broken.

Having a security blanket for your decisions isn't only unnecessary; it's harmful because it trains you to lack confidence. Confident people don't ask for permission.

All behaviors have consequences, but very few of them carry significant consequences. The harmless results people worry about are embarrassment or rejection. Sending four emails in a row, for example, could be embarrassing or cause the other person to reject your proposal. But if you're that persistent, perhaps it will make you stand out. It's best not to worry about it; if you want to do it and have a good reason to do it, do it.

Being rejected can make you feel dejected, but remember that rejection and failure are limited to one context: by that person, in that time, in that way, or in that category. An instance of rejection should never be seen as predictive for all future instances.

Embarrassment

Embarrassment doesn't help us much. Can you think of a specific way that being embarrassed has improved your life? Embarrassment's function is to discourage us from doing things to cause more embarrassment, but that's circular reasoning. Pain makes us avoid future pain, but that serves an important function to protect us. If you feel pain and continue to do what caused it, you will experience serious and possibly permanent physical impairment, because pain means you're damaging your body! Embarrassment, though, has very little downside other than the discomfort itself of feeling embarrassed.

This means that when you remove the feeling of embarrassment, there is no longer a problem. The only possible downside to doing embarrassing things (as long as you don't harm others) is alienating other people, but it's okay to alienate some people if that's what it takes to live life on your terms (and it often does).

This idea of needing to feel embarrassment to "protect your reputation" is so far to one extreme that it's a moot point. I say that because most people are at the other extreme. Why else would a significant number of people be too afraid to dance at venues where dancing is expected and encouraged?

Have you seen people do embarrassing things in public? How did they make you feel? Did you laugh? Deep down, were you jealous a little bit that they had the guts to do something so crazy without needing permission?

It's very desirable to have a desensitized embarrassment reflex, because it brings you freedom. The "crazy" people of the world have that going for them—they're not worried about being embarrassed. But most of us are so tame in our behavior that we'd never approach really embarrassing behavior even if we felt free to do it.

If you think I'm pushing you to run down your street naked, well, no. I'm saying that embarrassment itself is not something to fear. But you will fear it unless you get embarrassed more often. A perfectionist can only overcome perfectionism by practicing imperfect action. The reason for that is habit. We're most comfortable with how we've traditionally lived.

Imagine if you had to walk onto a stage in your underwear in front of 300 people and dance for five minutes. Aside from the "interesting" people who might enjoy that sort of thing right away, most people would find it unbearably embarrassing. But what if you did it every day for a year? At the end of the year, and as crazy as it may sound, I bet you would be moderately comfortable—if not completely comfortable—doing it.

Don't seek permission or fear embarrassment unless it involves something illegal or harms someone else. Otherwise, be yourself. But how can that be done? Like everything else, it's done with practice. Rebellion practice.

Rebellion Practice

The logical way to overcome the need for approval is to do things that others don't approve of. No, you don't have to break the law or do anything terrible to people. Rebellion is often associated with parties, illegal substances, and irresponsible living, but that's a specific type of rebellion—rebellion against authority. As kids, we're constantly under someone's immediate authority, being handed off from parents to teachers to coaches, so we tend to associate rebellion with authority.

Rebellion is broader than that.

- You can rebel against your typical way of living.
- You can rebel against societal expectations.
- You can rebel against peer pressure.
- You can rebel against any standard or expectation.

Those who have a strong need for approval are not rebels. They struggle to live in their own way because they try to attach everything they do to a standard practice. Or they try to live in the way that will draw the least amount of criticism from others. They need to rebel against their own need for approval, and they need to practice. When you don't care about the approval of others, you are free to be yourself and do things you'd never consider otherwise.

Need for approval can be widespread or specific. You may want approval from specific people, or from society as a whole, or both. For a shy single guy, the problem might be that he wants approval from women before he makes a move. If he tells a woman how he feels, she may not feel the same way, which is saying that she doesn't approve of him as a potential mate or that she doesn't approve of his approach.

Don't confuse rebellion with being a jerk or being insensitive. Those traits can go along with it, but all it essentially means is that you don't let others control your behavior. Wearing a fanny pack in the 21st century is rebellion.

You will never please everyone, and to even try to please a specific group doesn't make sense, because being yourself will naturally please some and alienate others. You'll accomplish that without trying.

Needing approval is a violation of your identity. This truth points to another truth: those who need approval don't know who they are. If you know who you are, it's much easier to live as yourself. If you're not sure who you are—maybe you're young or have followed others for too long—you'll look for your identity outside of yourself.

Don't seek approval from others or you'll never have approval from yourself.

This is easier said than done. You can't exactly find your identity overnight after not having one for years. But you can take the prerequisite step to find out—rebel. Rebel against whatever is putting your life on rails. It's only once you're free to make your own choices that you'll discover who you really are.

Action: Think back on your choices and how your need for approval has impacted them. Is it tied to a person who likes to peer into your life and judge you? Is it tied to a group of family or friends whose respect you desire? Or is it a general insecurity about fitting into society's expectations for a person in your position?

Your plan of rebellion needs to match your current need for approval. Personally, I am most sensitive to general societal expectations and judgments. So my rebellion practice involves things like lying down in public (I've done it), dancing like a fool (do it all the time), talking to women (getting better at it), and any other potentially embarrassing activity. Without fail, after doing one of these things, I feel extremely empowered. That's no coincidence, because I just demonstrated to myself and the world around me that I'm not controlled by it.

If your need for approval is tied to a specific person or group, identify some specific ways that he/she/they impact your behavior artificially. For example, are you embarrassed about what your friends would say about the job you really want to have? Is your desired path different than what your parents would approve of? (In these cases, it's often trickier, because nobody wants to upset Mom.) How to handle these is a case-by-case situation where you weigh your relationship with the person to the activity or activities that their influence keeps you from. How would rebellion affect the relationship and is it worth it?

If you want to get serious about overcoming perfectionism, and need for approval is a root cause, then create a mini habit of rebellion and practice it every day. It doesn't have to be too difficult.

If, at this point, you know you struggle with need for approval, but you're not sure what kind of rebellion would suit your situation, I recommend general practice.

Broader societal rebellion practice can help for personal situations, because it teaches you *how* to rebel. It might be a good stepping stone if you know you need to change your lifestyle in a way that will disappoint others. And again, don't just think of "bad things" here. Disappointing others can mean anything from marrying a poor person to getting a job outside of family tradition, and a million other harmless, unexpected choices that you may feel judged for.

Here are some general rebellion ideas.

Pose confidently in public. This is a nice two-for-one action combo. Combining Cuddy's confidence research with rebellion means you can spread your arms wide like a bird in public for two benefits. First, you'll chemically increase your confidence levels. Second, you'll look ridiculous in public, which is great rebellion practice.

Sing in public. Have you ever seen people sing randomly in public? Admittedly, I've judged those people, but they don't care. They're having a good time and enjoying life. This is a great way to practice rebellion because it's really easy to do (physically, not mentally), embarrassing, and funny. If you're terrible at singing, that's a good reason to laugh. People may think you're crazy, but that's part of this. If people think you're crazy, it shows they don't approve of you. Most people will just think you're being funny.

Lie down in public for 30 seconds. I heard of this idea from author Tim Ferriss, who talks about it in his bestselling book, *The 4-Hour Workweek*. He suggests doing this as a way to expand your comfort zone; its subtle brilliance is the fact that, for some reason, one of society's unstated rules is "thou shalt not lie on the floor in the presence of others for no reason," but at the same time, doing it harms no one and isn't illegal. It's a safe, yet effective way to challenge the ever-pressing will of society to control your behavior. I'd recommend doing it in a mall or store. A variation I like to do is public push-ups. Drop down in the middle of anywhere and crank them out. I recently did this in a crowded bar and a nearby group of people took a picture of me.

Wear a fanny pack. The younger you are, the more hilarious it will be.

Talk to strangers. For some people, including myself at times, it can feel like it isn't okay by social norms to talk to strangers without a really good reason. This is patently false (as anyone who regularly talks to strangers will confirm). There's even a study that suggests small talk with strangers makes us happier.[38] The study tested solitude versus socializing on public transit. Many participants claimed to prefer solitude, but they "reported a more positive (and no less productive) experience when they connected than when they did not."

A perfectionist will take this advice and then protest, "But what do I say to a stranger?" In answer, I'll refer you to your benchmark. If you're not confident in having a great conversation, say "Hi," and make that your success. If you think of something else to say, it's icing on the cake. If it feels awkward, it's great rebellion practice!

Walk in slow motion. This is another example of a harmless social behavior that will make people stare at you. It's easy to write it off and say, "That's stupid, what's the point?" Perhaps a more useful and interesting question is, "Why would something so trivial make people so uncomfortable?" The answer to that question is perfectionism. Society wants us to walk within a certain speed range and even look a certain way while doing it. Anything outside of this will be scrutinized, questioned, and judged.

It's ridiculous.

There's a pressure to conform. Always. This makes us all more susceptible to perfectionist tendencies. The aforementioned exercises are meant to challenge and reveal these ridiculous expectations placed upon us. People will think you're insane when you lie down in the middle of a public place or walk in slow motion, but is that really crazy? Perhaps. But it's even crazier for others to worry about it.

I'm not saying you won't ever need approval from people in your life. You will. For example, it's wise to want and work for your spouse's approval. The problem arises when your need for approval expands to everyone you come into contact with, and to such extremes with individuals or society as a whole that your true personality and personal preferences are smothered by incessant platitudes, expected actions, and play-it-safe living.

People tell each other to "Keep it real." What they should say instead is, "Lie on the floor for no reason." If you can do that, you're keeping it real, because you're demonstrating that you're comfortable flouting convention, at the cost of being judged.

If you can lie on the floor in the mall for 30 seconds, surely you can be yourself in a conversation or say "no" when the situation calls for it. Practice rebellion to detach yourself from the approval of the world, and in time, you'll be able live more freely.

(The more ridiculous these ideas sound to you, the more you would benefit from practicing them.)

Chapter 8

Concern over Mistakes

"Mistakes are a part of being human. Appreciate your mistakes for what they are: precious life lessons that can only be learned the hard way. Unless it's a fatal mistake, which, at least, others can learn from."

~ Al Franken

The Less-Than-Perfect Race

In 2008, the Big Ten Indoor Track Championship was taking place. One of the runners, Heather Dorniden, was favored to win the 600m sprint, which is three laps around the track. The runners were set and the gun sounded.

The race started out evenly. Then, toward the end of the second lap, Heather took the lead. But as she stepped in front of the second place runner, she tripped, literally falling into last place. The commentators felt sorry for her as she got up and started running again. "She's lucky she wasn't injured," one commentator said. "Her teammate just went to the front, though, so [the team] may be able to recover from that," said the other.

It was honorable that she decided to finish the race. But Heather didn't just finish the race, she *won* it. It's an incredible video to see. Some people will say its value is purely inspirational. When we see Heather trip, get up immediately, and give her best effort to win, it immediately triggers something within us that says, "This is what it means to be human."

But the lesson that sticks out to me is bigger than inspiration. Consider this:

the girl who won made more mistakes than any of the girls who lost.

Really think about that for a moment. The girl who won this race made a *huge* mistake; those who lost didn't make any noticeable mistakes. Too often, we assume that making a mistake means that we automatically lose, but usually it's just that they discourage us into a mindset that makes us lose. If Heather tripped, gave up hope, and lost, we'd all say she lost because she tripped. But since we know she was able to win the race despite tripping, that would have been a false assumption. If Heather gave up after tripping, she wouldn't have lost the race because she tripped; she would have lost because she let the trip discourage her from continuing to try. I'm sure she's glad she kept trying. It makes you wonder about the times you've given up too soon.

Winning isn't the result of tripping in the middle of a race, of course, but it is very often the result of persevering through mistakes.

How Concern Over Mistakes Impacts Us

Does concern over mistakes make people more likely to make them? Academic studies have been inconclusive. The study mentioned in chapter 3 found that perfectionists performed worse on a creative writing task, and this could be connected to concern over mistakes affecting creative performance. Two other studies found that concern over mistakes did *not* lead students to make more mistakes in an academic setting.[39] But one of those also found that it "can lead to perceptions of a more difficult course, higher anxiety, and a more negative mood."[40]

A statistical analysis on basketball player free throws could provide some insight. They found home teams are worse at free throws in clutch situations, but better at offensive rebounding.[41] A home player is likely to feel support from the home crowd, but they will also feel intense pressure not to make a mistake and disappoint their team and fans when the game is on the line. This causes them to focus inwardly and try harder, which can only distract them from making the free throw (a relatively simple fine motor skill).

Unlike shooting a free throw, where the game is at its slowest, battling for a rebound doesn't give a player *time* to worry about making mistakes. In the full-court game, they have no choice but to rely on their instinctual, subconscious-driven reactions. Additionally, failing to get an offensive rebound is not seen as a mistake so much as a missed opportunity.

Such research suggests that concern over mistakes may heighten our conscious awareness in a situation, which might impact the frequency of mistakes. Nevertheless, that is not the key concern.

Concerning yourself over making mistakes increases your anxiety and fear of action. The aforementioned research began with participants taking action. The players took free throws, and the students took tests, whereas you or I could be so concerned about making a mistake that we won't make an attempt.

We can't discern from these studies and statistics the *motivational impact* of concern over mistakes before action is taken, only afterwards. This makes the studies interesting, but less relevant to most of us whose problem is inaction because we fear making a mistake. Perfectionism researchers Hewitt and Flett succinctly say the truth of the matter: "Few activities are engaged in where the perfectionist is not assured of performing excellently."[42]

Before we get to the solutions for this, let's talk about *why* people concern themselves over mistakes. One key reason is known as Impostor Syndrome.

Impostor Syndrome

If you have significant concern over making mistakes, you may have Impostor Syndrome, which could be considered a sibling of perfectionism. In psychology, Impostor Syndrome is when someone is outwardly successful, but inwardly, they "experience secret intense feelings of fraudulence in achievement situations."[43] This creates a situation in which a person can appear and be successful, but still feel like an impostor.

A study found that "impostors" of this definition were more sensitive to mistakes and had more anxiety associated with such mistakes than others. Impostor Syndrome doesn't mean that you're an impostor—it only means you feel like one. For example, if you feel below your job's qualifications or prestige, you have Impostor Syndrome. Some of the most successful people have Impostor Syndrome *because* of their success.

Even the great Albert Einstein showed signs of Impostor Syndrome, perhaps because people said things like "the great" before saying his name. Just a month before he died, he told Queen Elisabeth of the Belgians: "The exaggerated esteem in which my lifework is held makes me very ill at ease. I feel compelled to think of myself as an involuntary swindler."[44]

Einstein's "perfect image" wasn't created by him, but bestowed upon him by society; seeing himself through the public's eye made him feel uncomfortable. This is often how it begins. Einstein knew he made mistakes; he had problems; and yet, his mind and his work were nearly worshipped for their profundity. This unrealistic image makes people feel like impostors and causes them to fear that making a mistake will show the world the truth.

Think about the labels and titles that society has placed on you, implicitly or explicitly, and how they have affected your belief of how you measure up. Back when I was a jobless undergraduate, I actually had the opposite of Impostor Syndrome. I felt that I was more qualified and capable than my jobless status and lack of callbacks suggested. Since writing *Mini Habits*, I've felt more like an impostor because of its success and the positive feedback I've received.

Why has Einstein's mind been so revered? And why are his accomplishments special? The reason his work was and still is held in high regard is *because* he was an imperfect person like the rest of us. If he and everyone else were perfect, and we all understood the entire world with great ease, then there'd be nothing to marvel at, would there? **It's only when we think we're required to be perfect that what we do seems trite.**

The odd thing about impostors is that they'll openly disclose their imperfections to others. They care about specific instances of performance, but not so much about how perfectly they present themselves. They may even be motivated to deflate their bloated public image.

"Thompson et al. (2000) found that Impostors have a higher level of fear of negative evaluation than non-Impostors and the motive behind their achievement behavior is to meet their perception of other people's standards."[45]

Impostors gauge what they think others' standards are in a particular area (but they tend to overestimate them), and they feel inadequate in comparison. Here's how Impostor Syndrome is connected to hindering action:

"They also strived to conceal their imperfection by not engaging in situations when they were likely to reveal their personal limitations to others. These characteristics found in Impostors were similar to those found in perfectionists, who are highly self-conscious and have a strong desire to conceal their mistakes from others in order to appear perfect (Frost et al., 1995)."[46]

If you're successful in the eyes of the world, remember that human accomplishments are only impressive because we are all flawed (otherwise, success would be ordinary). When you see life in that light, it takes the pressure off of you to measure up to a perfect image. If you think people expect perfection from you, take comfort in the fact that most people *don't care* what you do.

"Be who you are and say what you feel, because those who mind don't matter and those who matter don't mind."
~ Dr. Seuss

The difference is your focal point, which anchors your perspective:

- **Imperfectionists see and accept themselves as imperfect, which makes any and all success seem great.**
- **Perfectionists strive for their perfect ideal image, which makes any and all success seem like trash.**

For people with Impostor Syndrome, measuring accomplishments against their perfect ideal can become habitual, which means that all achievements are viewed with a negative bias. The solution, then, is to focus on the real you. The one with flaws. Forget your "image." The real you is your baseline, and mistakes are a part of that; they are normal and expected, not surprising.

The solution is not to ignore your flaws or even to focus elsewhere. It's only when you embrace your flaws as friends that you truly conquer their stranglehold on your confidence and perspective.

Is Impostor Syndrome Only for Successful People?
Though we've made a connection between success and Impostor Syndrome, one need not be successful to experience it:

"Harvey (1981) asserted that anyone can view themselves as an impostor if they fail to internalize their success and this experience is not limited to people who are highly successful."[47]

There are people who feel like impostors just for being loved. They don't believe they deserve it, and think that if they make a mistake, they will be exposed and lose it. They may think being loved is contingent on being the perfect spouse, friend, or father, which they know they cannot sustain.

Aside from consciously deciding to focus on the real you, the best way to combat Impostor Syndrome is to internalize your successes by writing them down. When you do this, remember that you're flawed, and it will magnify your sense of success rather than diminish it.

Action for Impostor Syndrome: Write down your accomplishments, the greatest things you've done or become. You can keep a digital or physical notepad to write them down on, and, whenever you feel like an impostor, consult your ongoing achievement list. Making this list is a worthwhile investment of your time, because it can be done in minutes and benefit you for a lifetime. Even if you don't suffer from Impostor Syndrome, an achievement list is useful. Continue to add to your list as you reach new heights. It can also serve as a progress report (include the date of the accomplishment to get a picture of your life's trajectory).

Impostor Syndrome is a subset of concern over mistakes, just as concern over mistakes is a subset of perfectionism. We're going to zoom back out now to concern over mistakes, which can be as simple as fearing mistakes for their own consequences. Other considerations aside, mistakes aren't enjoyable to make. It's not unreasonable to want to avoid them for that reason alone, but such a choice tends to result in a passive, boring, and unfruitful life.

Back to Einstein. Considering the amount of work he did, he didn't seem to be slowed down by a concern for making mistakes. He clearly had some degree of Impostor Syndrome later in life, but he may not have had it in his working years, or, if he did, it didn't seem to affect his productivity. Little to no fear of making mistakes is a trait of "doers," which Einstein was. In fact, this was his thought on making mistakes: "Anyone who has never made a mistake has never tried anything new."

Our behavior is a function of fear and desire. Those who have stronger fear than desire have a difficult time taking actions to improve their lives. As his statement suggests, Einstein's strong curiosity and desire for discovery were stronger than his fear of making mistakes. It's like seeing a dense fog in the woods: danger may lurk behind it, but the allure of its mystery still draws in the curious ones. However, not everyone has such a strong "pull of curiosity" and desire to break new ground as Einstein did.

How, then, can we non-Einsteins overcome the fear of making mistakes, reduce the associated anxiety, and take action with confidence?

The big question is whether we should try to lower our fear, increase our desire, or both, in order to make this equation work in our favor. If this were another book, I'd probably try to motivate you (increase your desire) at this point. Or I'd tell you to both face your fears and reach for your dreams! But those strategies fail in practice—"facing your fears" because it's a superficial treatment of a deep-seated perspective and motivation because it's fleeting.

If you have something that prevents action and something that enables action, is it most sensible to increase the enabler? Of course not! The logical solution in most cases is to *remove* the barrier. If you don't tackle your underlying fears, they will always be there to sabotage you, no matter how motivated you are to succeed.

Let's not treat fear casually. Let's respect our fear as a warrior respects a worthy enemy. Instead of going the route of increasing desire, we're going to use a strategy to reduce fear. It's a three-pronged tactical approach that cuts to the heart of fear and naturally trains us to not be afraid.

We'll start with binary thinking: not only is it extremely effective and easy to apply, but it's more fun than it sounds and it could very well be the "golden nugget" you take away from this book.

The Binary Mindset

This may be my favorite tool in the entire book.

Decreasing your fear of making mistakes starts with a perspective shift. But this isn't a matter of saying, "Choose to not fear the mistake." That kind of vapid advice is not useful, because, were it so easy, we'd all have done it already. The binary mindset is as simple as that advice, *but it's also easy to implement. Mini Habits* has proven that solutions need not be overly complex to bring great results.

This concept is the most exciting one I've come up with since mini habits, and it has had a profound positive impact on my life personally. Now that I've raised your expectations more than is wise, let's delve into the binary mindset!

The Binary Mindset
Binary is the language of computers, and it consists of only two characters—0

and 1. The digital technology that dominates today is based in binary language.

TVs receive digital or analog signals (newer TVs and broadcasts are all digital now). A digital TV signal is essentially binary data that is transformed into an image. If a digital signal is weak, but the data still gets through, it's a perfect picture. But if an analog signal is weak, the picture quality is too.

Digital/binary information is finite and defined information, while analog runs along a spectrum of practically infinite possibilities. How does this relate to our behavior?

One problem people have with stopping perfectionism is that *they like the idea of perfection*. Perfection is extremely desirable, which is why perfectionists are going to love the binary mindset. This mindset will enable us to use our desire for perfection to beat this subset of perfectionism (not wanting to make mistakes). If we were to turn digital and analog TV signals into a metaphor for tasks, here's what we'd get: Analog tasks can't be done perfectly. Binary tasks and concepts can be done perfectly. For analog to be perfect, the signal must be perfect as well, but binary can be perfect even with a weak signal. Let me give you an example of each.

Common binary task: Imagine your task is to flip a switch to turn the light on in your room. If you do it, it's done. It's perfect. Even if you trip and hit your knee and fall, but still hit the switch, you succeeded in your objective of turning the light on, and there's no middle ground. The switch is either on or off. In true binary form, the up position is "one" and the down position is "zero." Notice that the focus here is on *if* you've done the task, not *how well* you've done it.

Common analog task: If your task is to deliver a speech, it will not be done either flawlessly or 100% terribly, but somewhere in between those extremes. You might say the wrong word, perform one awkward gesture, and pause too long in any moment. You could stutter while saying something profound, or smoothly deliver a painful cliché. The speech may go well or not overall, but, whatever happens, it's going to be a mixed, analog result. Notice that the focus here is the opposite of the switch example: you're concerned with *how well* you're doing it, not *if* you're doing it.

Those examples are the "stereotypes" of each type of task. But watch what happens when we flip them around. This is important because it shows the way we perceive tasks is a choice (and that's a good thing, as you'll see!).

Typically binary example turned analog: Imagine your task is to flip a switch, but you have to do it in a certain way to consider it successful. You decide your finger must be perfectly parallel with the switch, and the precise moment that you flip the switch, you must be airborne doing a split while saying the word "pasta" in the 7th octave (please send me the video). Now you've made this typically binary task into an analog task. Even a successful flick of the switch can be marred—slightly or majorly—by performance mistakes. And think about this: in trying to meet all of these fancy requirements, you might actually fail to flip the switch!

Typically analog example turned binary: Imagine your task is to deliver a speech in front of 5,000 people. Most people would be thinking in analog terms here, because the speech could go from well to poorly or anything in between. But what if you decided that getting up on the stage and talking qualified as success? That's it. If you get on stage and say words, you succeed. Now, the only way to fail is to not say anything. Even if your speech is full of mistakes, you achieved the one and not the zero. A perfect success!

Which perspective do you think is the one of the perfectionist? Perfectionists are fully in the analog camp, because they want the details to be perfect. But the wonderful thing about binary tasks is that they *can* be accomplished perfectly. To become an imperfectionist in the area of not worrying about mistakes, create binary tasks for yourself, because they can easily be done "perfectly."

Usually, perfectionists are encouraged to accept imperfection as a means to change, but the best way to make it work in this case is to redefine what perfection means to you. And with binary tasks, this can be done in a logical way. It's not irrational to see giving a speech in front of 5,000 people as a perfect success. Doing it, regardless of the outcome, is a significant accomplishment.

"Perfect" describes things, and so when people say they're perfectionists, they mean that they tend to aim for perfection in many areas. But even when these areas are defined, such as "perfectionist writer," it's still too vague. Are they aiming for perfect grammar? Perfect sentence structure? Perfect storytelling? Perfect *everything*? Everything can't be aimed for unless you define exactly what constitutes *everything*. This kind of vaguely "perfect" aiming is the common, oxymoronic, and ironic misfire of the perfectionist. Binary simplifies the aim for perfection into something concrete and possible. That's why it's so satisfying—you get the satisfaction of perfectly meeting an objective that's entirely doable.

Binary Mindset in Action
The upcoming example is a different angle of the same strategy I used in the need for approval section, called "customizing your benchmark" (in which I only say "Hi" to women). Here's why: I feared making mistakes around women *because* I wanted their approval.

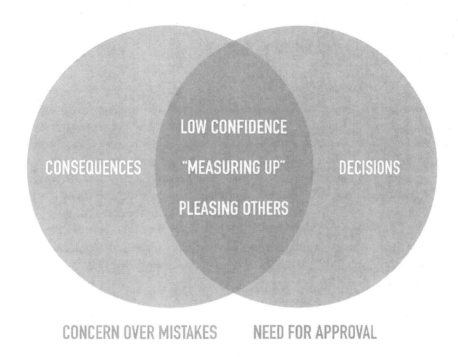

CONCERN OVER MISTAKES   NEED FOR APPROVAL

You can see the strong connection between needing approval and concerning yourself over mistakes. Increasing your confidence usually helps with both issues: when confident, you need less approval and are more assured in your ability to perform (and mistakes bother you less if you're confident). In practice, there's only a subtle difference between adjusting your confidence benchmark and creating a binary situation. The main difference is focus—a benchmark adjustment is for improving confidence and the binary mindset is for reducing fear.

My case was in the overlap area, so let me tell you how the binary mindset helped me.

I've historically been shy and perfectionistic when it comes to women, with a fear of making mistakes—saying the wrong thing, sending the wrong message, offending them, looking bad, etc. My breakthrough moment was when I changed to the binary mindset. I can pinpoint the exact moment that was the turning point for me.

One day, I was in a grocery store, and I saw a woman who took my breath away. This is the type of woman I wouldn't dare speak to, because the stakes were too high and I assumed I'd mess up in some way. But I had been thinking about this binary concept for some time, and I knew I needed to test it out. I created a binary objective that I could meet:

If I say "Hi" to her = 1.
If I don't do it = 0.

This was fascinating to me, because not only was the task easy (forcing myself to say one word), but also, *for the first time in my life, I had no pressure to be Dr. Smooth with a follow-up conversation thread*. I could get my win and literally run out of the store if I wanted to. So I forced myself to walk over to her, made eye contact, and squeaked out a "Hi." She seemed a little bit surprised and said "Hi" back. I did not say anything else and kept walking. Was it strange? You bet! Was she confused? Of course! Did I still succeed? I did.

I knew it wasn't technically perfect, but it didn't matter. I won. Like a weak digital signal that still results in a perfect image, my weak "Hi" was a perfect success.

As I smiled inside at this small victory, I pretended to look at the bulk foods. Interestingly enough, she came within a few feet of me shortly after. I think my one-word conversation piqued her interest, so I asked her how she was doing and we had a pleasant but short conversation. I didn't ask for her number, and I was definitely nervous, but the whole conversation itself was a bonus. Today, I am significantly better at talking to women and asking for numbers, and I have the binary mindset to thank for that.

To further clarify what a binary task is and the freedom it can give you, here are several examples of tasks we often see as analog that we can make binary and reap considerable rewards.

Deliver a speech: What if you could give the worst speech anyone has ever heard and still count it as a success? You can, if you think in binary terms! And why shouldn't you? Giving a speech is not something most people are naturally going to be superb at doing. It takes practice.

I've long said that I'm a better writer than speaker, and that's true, but I almost always say "yes" to podcast interviews. The moment I say "yes," and again after the interview, I consider it a success. Through a dozen or so interviews now, I've gotten *300 times* better than my (painfully) poor first few attempts, although I still have a *lot* of room for improvement.

If I had thought about the interviews in an analog way from the start, considering my performance, I would have never accepted the first interview. Or if, by some chance, I had accepted the first interview with an analog mindset, I would have ruminated on it and never accepted another interview (because it was really bad).

Taking a test: There are multiple ways to make test-taking a binary task. It is mostly about preparation, so you can start by counting X hours of studying as success or X amount of time on each page of study material (rather than worrying so much about how much you will retain). For the test itself, a "do your best and fill in every answer" attitude is the winning approach. If you do your best on each question, you've succeeded. But what if you fail the test? Worrying wouldn't change that result, so don't worry!

Being social: Socializing is one of the highest-stakes activities we engage in, because if we fail at connecting with human beings, we'll feel lonely and as if we have no place in the world. With such diversity on earth, everyone can find people they connect with if they keep trying and keep looking.

If you're shy, I've got a new rule for you. When you believe you should be social, but you're scared, all you have to do is point your face toward people and speak words. You may be a bumbling fool, but you just did something important—you practiced. Shy people will spend a lifetime trying to learn "the perfect way" to converse instead of practicing. "Point your face at them and speak" is simple and effective. The more you do it, the more feedback you'll get on how to express yourself and relate to others, the more comfortable and skilled you'll be at conversing.

As I said before, my shyness has mostly been in relation to women. Now look at the difference binary thinking made to my thought process.

As a perfectionist: What should I say to her first? She knows she's pretty, and complimenting her will just make me seem like every other guy. But I want to be nice and show her I'm attracted to her. But that will make me seem desperate. Maybe I should playfully tease her? What should I say, though? I don't want to use a pick-up line. But those are funny and she might like it. I wonder how awkward it would be to talk to her. Oops, she left five minutes ago.

As an imperfectionist: If I talk to her, I win. I'll say "Hi."

Freedom is walking up to a woman, tripping over your shoes, coughing three times, stuttering on your first word, and after this medley of mistakes, talking to her and calling it a success.

The other benefit of this is focus. Often the reason we get flustered is because of the innumerable variables to consider and what may go wrong (analog thinking). What should I say to her? What if I embarrass myself? What if she already has a boyfriend and I'm wasting my time? These are all unknowable details, and that's why they truly *don't matter* when it comes to taking action. Let's stop making assumptions and take action to figure things out in real time by using the binary mindset.

Not All Mistakes Are Equal
It might sound strange, but one of the best examples of a binary task is doing laundry. I'm pretty terrible at doing laundry. I always seem to let clothes drop on the floor when unloading from the dryer. Just recently, I finished my laundry and put the basket back in its spot, only to see a dirty sock on the floor! I missed it. **I made a mistake.**

Why don't people feel emotionally destroyed inside after the mistake of dropping a sock? Because not all mistakes are equal, but why is that?

It's not the concept of making a mistake that bothers us (dropping a sock, your finger missing the switch, etc.). Our fear is that certain mistakes will define who we are. Of course, this fear is misguided, because as Heather Dorniden demonstrated when she won that race, it's not our mistakes that define who we are and shape our future, it's our response to them.

While not all mistakes *feel* the same, our *response* to them should be the same— learn and keep moving. Maybe one day I'll be able wash all of my socks, but even if not, I'm going to continue washing my clothes.

Why Simplicity Crushes Perfectionism and Fear
Binary tasks simplify your objective (flip the switch = 1, give the speech = 1, don't = 0); perfectionists' fear causes them to drown in complexity. Considering all of the possible ways a mistake could be made takes a lot of mental effort. This "works" for them because the overwhelming pressure and increased fear from visualizing everything that could go wrong drives them to a safer activity, where relief is found (until they're reminded again). Can you see why perfectionism is the root cause of procrastination?

Procrastination is not caused by laziness but by a combination of

fear and overcomplicated objectives, which come from a perfectionistic mindset.

The binary mindset is at the heart of imperfectionism and is a powerful way to dissolve your concern over mistakes. It's structured in such a way that mistakes won't feel like mistakes. It is empowering because it competes with "excuse" activities like watching TV; it takes away excuses while simplifying action to encourage you forward.

Using exercise as an example, you don't need to have a "good" workout. This removes excuses like low energy, poor equipment, bad timing, the wrong location, and more. Excuses rarely mean something is impossible, they mean it's not ideal. If you nix your need for a "good" workout, you make it excuse-resistant. From there, the encouraging "just show up to win" sentiment nudges you forward.

Binary focuses on facts—did it happen or not? The analog, subjective component focuses on quality, impact, reception, mistakes, and overall, how close to perfect it was. Always choose binary, and through learning and practice, you'll get the desired results without worrying about them.

Create a New Path of Least Resistance

Generally, people think of mistakes as regression, but as an imperfectionist with binary thinking, mistakes that happen on your way to getting a "1" are an acceptable part of the process. I want to hammer in a concept that can change your life: **those who simplify and make success easier than failure are those who get into "success cycles."**

Most commonly, you'll look around and see people in cycles like depression-inactivity-depression-inactivity, guilt-overeating-guilt-overeating, or tired-lazy-tired-lazy. These negative cycles are prevalent because they're the default paths of least resistance. They're easy to get into, and we like the easy way. That's why making success easier transformed my life (and the lives of many others who have read *Mini Habits*).

For all of humanity's merits, you can't deny that we love the path of least resistance. Sure, we take the hard path sometimes, but it costs us a bucketful of energy and willpower! I live in the USA, and our entire society is based around making everything easier. Washing machines let us throw our clothes into a magical box and they come out clean. Dishwashers let us throw nasty dishes into another magical box and they come out clean. Microwaves are magical boxes that give us meals in minutes. TVs are magical boxes that let us experience exciting lives vicariously through others. Magical boxes are popular here because they make life easier.

We love easy. As such, forcing ourselves to do hard things won't last long because *we don't like it*; it works better to make the hard things easier to do. With this understanding, it's no longer shocking that my big breakthrough in fitness (and in life) happened when I "messed around" with doing one push-up a day. That was very easy, easy enough to do consistently. It destroyed my concept of what a workout was "supposed to" look like. Before long, my exercise perfectionism was annihilated.

The secret to consistent success that compounds over time is to combine small goals with the binary mindset: one push-up a day = (binary) 1 = success. The binary mindset reframes what success and perfection are to you, and the small goal makes the target so easy it's nearly impossible to resist.

The rich get richer; the lazy get lazier; the confident get more confident; the fit get fitter; and the fat get fatter. This is the way it most often works, and it's absolutely frustrating if you're on the wrong end of it. If you've struggled with negative cycles of depression, anxiety, eating, guilt, etc., then you already know the power of negative momentum. You know exactly how negative spirals can bring the strongest people to their knees in despair. I'm telling you that the exact same principle that traps people in those terrible cycles can be used to create upward success spirals.

Make success easier than failure, and you'll succeed.

Redefine Success as Progress (Modular Success)

The challenge in changing from perfectionist to imperfectionist is doing it in a way that doesn't feel like you're lowering your standards, which always seems wrong. Binary thinking is one way to redefine success, and here are some other useful ways to do it that result in more action, less fear, and ultimately a better life.

Imperfectionists are perfectionists in a unique way.

Instead of expecting perfect results, the imperfectionist expects perfect progress and consistency. What if you always made forward progress every day? What if your track record for daily progress was perfect? Even small or flawed progress gets significant very quickly when you're consistent.

Most people already realize the key to life is taking the right actions. That doesn't mean having a workaholic personality—it's broader than that. Taking action sometimes means watching a movie or taking a nap when you need to recharge. Relaxation is an important component of a balanced and well-lived life. The unfortunate alternative is passive living, where you "float" along and let life take you where you'd never choose to go on your own.

Progress Is Success

If I trip and fall forward, then I've still moved further than I would if I hadn't taken a step. If an action—however small or flawed—helps you, then it's good. This painfully simple truth is distorted in the mind of a perfectionist. I say that from experience as a former perfectionist.

Because of how perfectionists define success, they can perform 80 push-ups and feel like a failure because they missed their goal of 100. Their bodies benefit from the exercise, but their future progress is harmed by their perspective. When you berate yourself for imperfect performance, you *can* squeak out improved performance in the short term. This is why so many people do it. But in the long-term, you're damaging your sense of self-worth and competence. Even if the damage is minor, you have to compare it to what it's like to always appreciate forward progress.

The fuel of self-punishment won't last through the night, but the fuel of self-encouragement accomplished through a smart action strategy can last a lifetime.

I've found through practicing mini habits that an appreciation for all forward progress is life-changing. I've also noted that this mindset is rare. When a person adopts this mindset and practice, they systematically break down the barriers of "not good enough." It isn't lowering your standards, it's redefining success as progress and *raising your standards for consistency*.

When the truth of this sinks in, you'll genuinely be able to do a single push-up and feel good about it. After a lifetime of "normal goals," it's strange, but once you start, you will likely get hooked on the feeling of consistent daily success.

Modular Success Beats Chunk Success

In our lives, we're trained from birth by society to pursue success in chunks. In school, we study all semester and take the final exam, hoping to receive the big "A" afterward. After school, we go to job interviews and eventually are rewarded with the big job. We see others set goals to lose 50 pounds and hear all about it from the ones who reach it. It fools us into thinking that this is the nature of success—put in a ton of work up front and get the reward in one chunk payment.

This whole philosophy is brought down by this simple question: does doing a minimal amount of something make you more or less likely to do more of it? Lays potato chips had the slogan "Bet you can't eat just one," because it's not human nature to stop after a taste of success. Success to us is like blood to sharks! Lays understood that tasting a delicious chip is a form of success (reward) that makes us want to repeat the process. This is modular success.

Some people have come to believe that they need an accurately-sized goal *in order* to do something. They think that, in order to reach 20 push-ups, that "chunk" must be aimed for at the start. By now, *thousands* of people have proven this theory wrong by using mini habits. I've received *hundreds* of stories of people excitedly telling me how they regularly surpass their initially small aim.

Success is not naturally as "chunky" as society tends to make it appear. The natural identity of success is modular. Even if someone gets that "chunk success" moment, it may not be enough to fuel them to greater heights, as daily living requires a daily fuel source.

There's another factor at play here, which is autonomy (freedom). Autonomy means that you have control over your decisions and they mean something to you. When you set a lofty goal, you cede control to your goal and lose autonomy. You bow to the goal as your new master. Even worse, this goal is probably an arbitrary number or social norm—lose 50 or 100 pounds, go to the gym X days a week, go through a workout program. The goal becomes your parent, telling you that you can't skip your workout "because it says so." And you attempt to suck it up and cling to a stale decision you made a month ago.

Do you see how this is a minor form of self-punishment? Like all self-punishment, it can work for a time, but soon enough, a rebellion is likely, and your subconscious mind will be the one yelling and holding the pitchfork. As a kid, rebellion looks like a temper tantrum. As an adult, it looks like binge-watching TV, mindlessly wasting time online, and other ways to creatively avoid your goals.

Redefine success as progress, and success will become modular. You'll get more frequent feelings of accomplishment and create a powerful foundation that can always be added to.

Chapter 9

Doubts about Actions

"A good plan violently executed now is better than a perfect plan executed next week."

~ George S. Patton

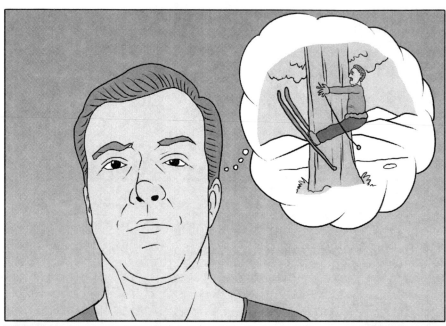

Choosing Experience over Projection

If a sliver of doubt exists about doing something generally or right now, what's the most likely response? Delay action until you're more certain.

Projection is the primary reason why people have doubts about actions. Projecting means predicting or imagining an outcome; it is often inaccurate. Have you noticed sometimes before doing something requiring effort that you will subconsciously project it as being exceedingly difficult and unpleasant? There's a reason for that.

The defining trait of the subconscious mind is that it does not like change, and it will try to influence our conscious thinking into agreeing with that stance; giving us inaccurate projections is one way it does that. I remember wanting to do a simple 30-minute workout one day, but then seeing it as overwhelming, too hard, and not worth it. When I started small with one push-up and built up to a 30-minute workout, I found that my initial projection was way off. Not only was it not very difficult, but it was enjoyable and felt highly rewarding afterwards.

When a perfectionist projects, there's big trouble, because their projections tend to be more unrealistic in the opposite direction of their perfect ideal. But even projecting realistic outcomes is a problem when you expect and desire perfection, as it means you won't want to take action. There's almost always a downside that can be seen when you project the outcome of any decision or course of action.

Let Experience Be Your Teacher
The problem with projection is that it's theoretical. You can project for a lifetime, but the only way to know for sure how something will go is to try it. Once you start experimenting, you'll find flaws in your initial projections. Look for them, and you'll be more likely to identify faulty projections in the future.

Every time I exercise, I compare the outcome to what I had projected, and to this day, the real thing is better every time. Now when I don't feel like exercising and I begin to project, I have a wealth of experience to combat it. For me, the projection tends to assume that my current energy level will be static through my workout. But in reality, when you begin to exercise and blood flow increases, it becomes much easier because your body "changes modes" from sedentary to active. This is the kind of thing that projectors rarely calculate, even if they know it's true!

People who have gone from shy to social—this includes me—did it by forcing themselves to socialize and get that experience. They gradually learned that it wasn't as scary as they always projected it to be.

Do you think I projected my first published book to become an international best seller? Absolutely not! I was confident in the value of the content, but while writing it, I had to deal with projections like: *I'm going to spend several months writing this book and very few people will buy it* and *if I don't get a regular job, I'll end up on the street.* I knew that the only way to know for sure was to write the most useful book I could, market it as best I could, and see what would happen. The result changed my life.

If you make an assumption like "I could never [insert dream job here] for a living," you won't ever try it. If you've already tried and failed, remember that all experience must be analyzed to determine its components of chance and failure. Most pursuits are chance-heavy and require multiple attempts to get right, so quitting after one negative result isn't justified just because you've experienced it.

Projection is common and easy to do, but it's a very poor substitute for getting out there and finding out for sure how things work.

For the biggest impact, write down projections as you make them. Then set out to experiment, and write down the actual result. I guarantee you, it will be fascinating to compare your projections to the actual results.

If you don't want to write anything down, simply be mindful of your projections and make mental notes of how you perceive tasks in important areas of your life. If you don't know where to begin, look for common areas of resistance such as exercise, work tasks, home chores, replying to email, reading, communicating in relationships, writing, practicing languages, or practicing instruments. Areas of resistance have the greatest potential for projection, because when you feel resistance, it means your subconscious wants something else, and it will project a biased outcome to plant a seed of doubt in your mind and get its way.

Sometimes projections are vague, like expecting to not enjoy something or expecting a negative result of no specific kind. Vague projections can be the worst because vague problems are always harder to solve than specific ones. But you can compare your vague projection to the result, and see how accurate they were.

It's possible that some of your projections will come true. If that's the case, then you at least know that you really do hate mowing the lawn (like me). Or if you really do hate exercising and still want to do it for good health, you have a lot more information to solve that problem. Pinpoint what it is about exercise that you don't like and develop a routine that minimizes those things.

The Procrastination Connection

If you have a doubt about taking action, what will you do next? Likely nothing. Procrastination is a common response to doubts about actions.

Everyone has a theory on procrastination:

* It's because we dread the work
* It's because we fill up the time we have (Parkinson's Law)
* It's because we're addicted to Candy Crush

The case-by-case reasons for procrastination vary, but individual reasons aren't all that helpful for solving the problem. Let's find the root cause of procrastination by examining how it works. First, we know that procrastination means that we've failed to make the decision to act, or that we've failed to act on the decision. The decision comes first, so we'll start there.

Procrastinators Get Stuck in Deliberation
Procrastination's most useful definition is: failure to enter the implemental phase.

In making decisions, first we deliberate (weigh our options) and then we implement (act). For doubts about actions, it's not always an issue of whether or not the action is a good idea—it's often an issue of making a decision. To take action on one thing means that you can't take action on anything else for that time. Knowing this, some people struggle to choose out of fear that they're not making the very best decision.

If you can commit to one task, your thinking switches to the implemental phase and you'll take action. The goal is to transition from deliberation to implementation. In the words of researchers Vohs and Baumeister:

"To move from the first mental mode to the second involves a termination of the deliberating process and then an initiation of actions in pursuit of the chosen option. [...] The philosopher Searle (2002) has discussed this difference at some length and argues that rationality presupposes some degree of free will (or purposeful control over behavior) because rational analysis is functionally useless unless one can act based on the outcome of the analysis. Searle further emphasized that people can recognize multiple reasons to behave in a certain way but still not perform the behavior, again indicating that contemplating and choosing are separable steps."

That's a bit wordy, but the root issue is that procrastinators fail to commit to a single course of (valuable) action. They don't leave the deliberative mindset. You could say that they've simply chosen other activities, but that carries the same implication of NOT committing to worthwhile tasks and selecting a default one instead.

This takes us to another question: why do procrastinators delay commitment to important things?

How Perfectionism and Fear Reverse Your Priorities

Perfectionism either leads to or is caused by fear, depending on the person. If you're scared, your fragile state of mind will want things to go perfectly (or not at all). Or if you are a perfectionist requiring the absolute best results, the pressure can scare you. Perfectionism and fear are happily married.

As the most important tasks to us are automatically the scariest ones, fear drives us to choose zero-risk and unimportant "filler" activities (i.e., it reverses our priorities). When your priorities are reversed, you might find yourself treating trivial games and social media like must-do activities and ignoring the things you really want to do.

Many people use perfectionism as an excuse; they wear it as a mask to disguise their fear. Under that mask is a person too scared to face the reality that imperfect action is all we have. (Note: I'm not talking about people with clinical OCD; that's another matter.)

Perfectionism can be a life-destroying problem when it reverses your priorities. Here's how it ties in with procrastination.

The pseudo-benefit of procrastination (i.e., staying in the deliberative mindset) is that it maintains the illusion of perfection. It's only when you pull the trigger and say, "I'm going to work on writing my book right now," that you're exposed to an entire wave of imperfection. Imperfections in this doubtful wave might include low energy levels, a lack of ideas for the book, not feeling motivated to write, bad timing, or low confidence in your ability to produce good work for any reason. Before action, it's seemingly possible that you could get in the perfect mood, have the perfect ideas, and produce a perfect result. But once you enter action, you're hit pretty hard with the imperfection of reality, and it's not fun.

Even though we all know it takes hard, "unpretty" work to do something meaningful, the perfection fantasy about our work and our lives can still persist because it's an emotional desire (not a logical one). In real life, conditions for work and results from said work are never perfect. For example, I wrote a portion of this chapter with an aggressively affectionate cat kneading my thighs ... and other areas. It was imperfect for productivity; it tickled and made me laugh, but I continued (as best I could).

One way to learn how to do something better is to observe someone who already does it well. Movie heroes are fearless in the face of sure death, but have you noticed how they don't procrastinate either?

Lessons from Hollywood
It turns out that the fearless nature of movie heroes and their non-procrastinating ways are intricately connected.

Does James Bond—as fearless as anyone—ever think, *hmmm, well ... um ... maybe we should ... no ... uh ... I don't know what to do.* No. He's making a quick, confident decision as I write this. Sometimes it's the wrong decision (imperfect!), and he suddenly finds himself with three guns pointed at his head, but guess what happens then? He is saved by the screenwriter. Okay, *deus ex machina* jokes aside, Bond *adapts and conquers*. And if you're going to be a true imperfectionist, adaptation is your weapon of choice! All it means is: you'll make it work.

Don't you get the sense that this is the key to life? Act, adapt, and conquer! It's so much more exciting and productive than standing still and waiting for the right sign to do something with a guarantee it's your best option.

If you're willing to make imperfect decisions and take imperfect action in imperfect conditions, you will conquer procrastination.

Embracing imperfection in all phases of the process destroys excuses. It kills the fear of failure because it includes failure as part of the process: "I know this won't go perfectly, but it will go."

The Tragedy of the Perfect Decision-Maker

I want to tell you a story of two young men. One is a perfect decision-maker (PDM) and the other is an imperfect decision-maker (IDM). IDM and PDM want girlfriends. Let's see what happens.

Round One
IDM walks up to a girl and asks her to be his girlfriend. She draws back and says "no."

PDM examines a girl from afar. He envisions a romantic gesture in which he swings in on a vine with a rose in his mouth, asking her to dance. As she begins to wonder who this hero is, she will turn around to see a live band. They will dance the night away as the sun slowly melts into the horizon. End scene.

Round one: PDM wins with no rejection and one of the nicest fantasy dates he's ever made up.

Round Two
IDM walks up to a girl and says, "Hello." She says, "Hi" and the conversation ends because she hurries away like she's late to meet the president.

PDM sees a girl and considers several clever phrases he could say:

- "I love your shoes." — No, it's too obvious that he's just trying to flatter her.
- "Nice weather today, isn't it?" — Absolutely not. Trite small talk is not going to impress her.
- "Have you been here before?" — That sounds like something a stalker would ask! Out of the question.

Round two winner: PDM. He avoided saying the wrong thing or having the girl walk away.

Round Three
IDM walks up to a girl and smiles. She smiles back and he holds her gaze. He

walks up to her and says, "Hi, how are you?" She says, "I'm well, and you?" "I'm better now," he says with a smirk. She slaps him in the face.

PDM sees a girl and smiles at her. The moment she looks up at him, he averts his gaze. "She caught me staring," he thinks, "or maybe she's interested, but if I look at her, she could definitely reject me. Maybe I need to wait until she looks at me first. You know what, though? I'm in a grocery store now, so this isn't a good place to meet someone anyway."

Round three winner: PDM wins with no slaps in the face.

After three rounds, let's look at the results. Wow! The perfect decision-maker is absolutely trouncing the imperfect decision-maker, who has made a number of embarrassing mistakes so far. Let's call game, set, and match, shall we? Oh. What's that? I hear people clamoring for another round. That's strange. We already know who's going to win! The PDM hasn't made a single poor decision yet! Ok, fine. Here's round four.

Round Four

A girl walks up to IDM and says, "Hey, I went to school at UVA, too. What year did you graduate?" They talk for a while and he's careful to learn from his past mistakes this time. He doesn't ask her to be his girlfriend right away and he doesn't make an offensive joke. He just decides to be himself and he can do it since he's now comfortable talking to girls. She gives him her number and they have a wonderful first date (those magic floaty things that were in *Avatar* were there).

A girl walks up to PDM and startles him by saying, "Hey, I went to school at UVA, too. What year did you graduate?" He struggles through the conversation because he's so nervous and unprepared to talk to a girl. In the thousands of simulations he's done, they never went quite like this. And in his nervousness, he makes quite a few out-of-character comments and comes across as an unconfident mess. She excuses herself because she has a meeting. Yeah, sure she does.

Round four winner: PDM with ... uh ... wait, WHAT? The IDM won this round? How is that possible?

It's possible because, while the PDM was busy making the perfect plan, the IDM was out there learning from real world experience. Perfect decision-makers have one huge problem with their strategy: **not even a perfect decision-making machine can make perfect decisions with imperfect data.** In order to make a perfect decision, the data the decision is based on must also be perfectly accurate. But the most important data is only found through imperfect experimentation. That's a conundrum for anyone who wishes to always make the right decision.

We think about good decision-making as if it's the holy grail of life, but the reason the imperfect decision-maker won in the end is not because he made better decisions. On the contrary, he made far more tangible mistakes that the perfect decision-maker did. But when you make a mistake that doesn't permanently harm you, it helps you. Every rejection or slap for the IDM gave him more information about how he presented himself, and made him more comfortable talking to girls. In retrospect, the poor choices he made were the best choices. And the same can be true in real life.

Exposure to any circumstance hardens your outer shell against feeling pain or intimidation from it. The guy who gets rejected by one girl every five years feels it way more than the guy who gets rejected every week. The woman who gives terrible speeches regularly feels it less than the first timer. That's just how our brains are wired. As psychologist Nico Fridja put it, "Continued pleasures wear off; continued hardships lose their poignancy."[48]

If you let any doubt stop you from acting, you will avoid living a meaningful life. But if you pursue the things you want as best you can, you'll figure things out. Trial and error is the time-tested way to improve something.

If someone struggles with doubts about their actions, what kind of skill can they develop to directly help? Earlier, we discussed how procrastinators have a difficult time leaving the deliberation phase, because they not only doubt their idea but also doubt it is the *best* idea right now. The action-based cure for this is simple—speed.

Making faster decisions is one of the most underrated skills of mankind. Like any skill, it can be practiced and developed to the point where you zip right past most of your petty doubts about important actions that can improve your life. Let's get into how to make faster decisions.

Make Faster Decisions

Decisions are hard because of all the variables involved: timing, difficulty, reward, risk, alternatives, and expectations. In the moment, it's deceptively complicated to decide between writing a story, exercising, and playing guitar.

The brain has a tough task to find distinguishing factors that make one of them a clear "best decision." And the battle doesn't always end there.

You might calculate that playing guitar is the best move right now, but remember the earlier discussion on deliberation and implementation, and how perfectionists get stuck deliberating over the "perfect choice"? **If you hesitate to move to implementation even briefly, you may loop back to deliberation and get lost in the details of complex variables.** Even worse, this can become habitual.

Instead of developing the habit of looping back to deliberation, you can develop the habit of having a quick trigger finger. You can be the person who is always looking to enter the implemental mindset. And really, this is where we're all trying to go. Implementation means action, and action means learning and progress, which lead to success.

Instead of suggesting blindly rushing into action, however, let's look at the line at which further contemplation does not benefit us anymore.

The second you understand there is a bigger benefit and less downside to doing something, do it. And do it right away unless you're in the middle of something else extremely important. Don't think about eating a snack first. Don't check Facebook first. Those things are mental debris; they can take you away from your initial thought and force you to go through the deliberation process again.

This is a key way to defeat procrastination. It's somewhat hard to explain as it takes place in the mind, but you'll be thinking, "Oh yeah, I guess I have time to work out." DECISION MADE. If you have time to work out, and you want to do it in general, there is no benefit in weighing it against the unlimited number of other things you could do. I've been practicing this lately and it's really helped me to take action early and often. One way to think of it is turning your brain off. Don't allow yourself to analyze further when it isn't necessary.

Vague Feelings of Risk (Are Usually Wrong)

Imagine a three-person gun standoff. They're each pointing guns at one another's heads. Do you think they should quickly move to action here? Probably not. If one person shoots, it's a decision that carries a lot of risk and potentially no reward; it could end one or more lives. In cases like this, deliberation is critical.

Switching back to scenarios in our lives, we're often making decisions about reading, writing, doing taxes, working out, and talking to a friend. These are all low-risk activities with a similar opportunity cost, which means it's almost impossible to choose wrong. I have never done my laundry and cried about it afterwards, needing a few days to process my grief. And yet, it's still easy to procrastinate doing it. Why?

When you put it all together, the answer is clear: **we (habitually) assume that, because our brains are amazing analytical machines, we should use them for every ... little ... tiny ... decision.**

It helps to have a powerful analytical brain when considering your marriage partner, weighing your mortgage options, or deciding on a career. It doesn't help much for the simple things.

How to Apply This Information and Destroy Procrastination
Be mindful about the true risk of choosing incorrectly. If it's between laundry and playing guitar, there is no wrong choice unless you're low on clean socks (a dire emergency). If it's between steak and salmon for dinner, I recommend salmon, but it's not worth wasting decision-making energy on it. If it's between dozens of things you could do with your free time, choose one of your *good* ideas and be happy about it.

To do this, you must:

- Embrace imperfection.
- Consider the true risk and consequences of doing the wrong thing (it's almost always zero, which removes pressure to "choose right").
- Simplify your thinking to stop overanalyzing each option. If activity = good, then do it. This level of thinking is caveman simple, but it's effective.

With the time and energy saved by moving to the implementation mindset as quickly and frictionless as possible, you'll be able to do more of ALL of the things you want to do. Decision-making is accomplished with the pre-frontal cortex, making it an energy-intensive task, so expediting the process will save you a lot of energy!

A Note about Deadline Procrastination
You may be thinking about instances when you have a project deadline. In this case, you have a clear objective with a timeframe, but too often, find yourself delaying action to the last minute. This is actually no different than what was just discussed. While you have a clear objective that you must get done by a certain date, you still don't have a clear *starting point*, and so it is

thrown into the mix with all other possible activities.

Here are two ways to overcome this problem.

Method 1: The short-term solution is to schedule it. Simple and effective.

Method 2: The long-term solution to this is to retrain yourself. The moment you think it might be a decent time to start working on it, do it (and terminate the deliberation process). Don't reconsider. Take action. With enough practice, this will become the new way of doing things. As a bonus, people who have the quick-decision habit are seen as fearless and confident.

Faster decisions are made easier when combined with lowering your standard for taking action, which we discussed in chapter 5 (unrealistic expectations). I read a blog article recently by a guy who wrote the entire post on his cell phone. He was on a bus, and was expected to post to the blog, but he didn't have his laptop. Most bloggers—including me—have a standard that says, "If I don't have my laptop, I can't write and publish a blog post." But because he lowered his standard for action, he was able to make a productive decision in non-ideal circumstances. If he had a stubborn standard for action, he may have wavered for a while over what to do, wasting his time and energy in the process.

The Two-Minute Rule
A great, actionable trick to cut down on inefficient deliberation is the two-minute rule. I read about this rule in David Allen's book, *Getting Things Done*. The rule is: if it takes two minutes or less, do it without further contemplation. Since deliberation requires so much cognitive energy (relying heavily on the analytical ability of the prefrontal cortex), inefficiency is a problem. This is a brilliant rule, because in that time frame, the time spent deliberating is *never worth it*.

Things that may take two minutes or less:

- Clear or vacuum your room floor
- Do any single phase of laundry (wash, dry, sort)
- Pour a glass of water
- Write and send an email
- Do any of your mini habits

Recap of how to make faster decisions:

1. Be mindful of true risk.

2. Always be looking to terminate the deliberation phase ASAP with a commitment to one task (this is aided by low action standards and looking for a "good" choice instead of "the guaranteed best" choice).
3. Follow the two-minute rule to eliminate worthless overanalysis.
4. Practice the above, and you'll be well on your way to breaking your procrastination habit by making faster decisions and taking action!

Mo Data, Mo Problems

Doubt causes a desire for more information. It's found in gray areas where more information could tip the scales one way or the other. This scenario is what makes procrastination feel productive sometimes.

If you feel the need for more information about a decision, you might wait to make it. There are two possibilities here:

1. More information can be obtained to make the decision easier.
2. More information can't be obtained, or won't impact the decision.

When you find yourself delaying and doubting, ask yourself which of these scenarios it is. In truth, delaying a decision is **never** the right choice. That's because, even if you need more information to decide, you can decide in that moment to *seek* new information. And if new information will not help your decision, you're best off to make it right then and there. Either way, you're making a proactive choice rather than delaying.

Say you're considering starting a garden. The non-urgency of the task can make you feel like you have plenty of time to start it later. In addition, there are many initial steps and tips about gardening you'd like to know before you begin. The combination of these two—too little information and too much time—can easily keep your garden a dream instead of something in your backyard.

My preferred solution is to start and see what happens.

In 2011, I had this problem. I wanted to have a website or blog to share my thoughts, but I had the rest of my life to start it and had very little information or preexisting knowledge about where to begin. I ended up jumping in and learning as I went along. I knew the first step was to register a domain, so I registered deepexistence.com. This set everything in motion. I learned, I experimented, and I blogged. Four years later, that decision has changed my career path.

Risk, Reward, and Probability

Generally speaking, we need less information than we think we need to make decisions. Those who constantly seek information might have a confidence problem. Confidence is going into an unknown situation and believing that you'll come out of it alright. It's trusting yourself, not to always make perfect decisions, but to be able to adapt to changing circumstances as needed.

In rare cases, you'll need more information and research, but for everything else, run through these questions:

1. What's the worst thing that could happen? How likely is that to happen, and could I recover from it?
2. What's the best thing that could happen? How likely is that to happen, and how nice would that be?
3. What's most likely to happen?

You can use a 10-point scale to rate the outcomes, with 10 being the most extreme in each case. If the potential upside is a 10 and the potential downside is only a 4, it's probably a good idea! This makes the risk and reward more defined and it's an easy way to give yourself more information to make a decision.

Garden example:

1. WORST CASE: 7/10 — After dozens of hours of work, a natural disaster or infestation would ruin it. Or I'd start the garden and realize I don't have time to keep up with it. CHANCE: Unlikely — It's unlikely to happen, and while it would be tough, I'd be fine, and would still retain knowledge about gardening and learn from the experience.
2. BEST CASE: 9/10 — I'd have a beautiful garden with fresh, healthy vegetables and very few problems! CHANCE: Possible — It seems possible with the right preparation. I can't resist homegrown squash.
3. MOST LIKELY OUTCOME — A garden with occasional problems with pests and weather that still yields nice vegetables.

Most people only have a vague idea of the risk and reward of decisions, which makes it difficult for them to gauge if it's a worthwhile pursuit, and often causes them to seek new information to make sure they don't make a mistake. But Einstein pointed out the flaw in that when he said, "Anyone who has never made a mistake has never tried anything new." You can't try new things with complete assuredness that you're doing the right thing.

Quantity over Quality

Is quantity or quality more important? That depends on what we're talking about. In many cases, people automatically assume quality to be better, but when it comes to making decisions and taking action, quantity wins.

The most successful people (however you wish to define success) are not the ones who get it right the first time. They're the people who struggle and learn through experience.

Almost every successful businessman you talk to will have stories of failed businesses, terrible ideas, and other not-so-impressive shortcomings. All of the following men went bankrupt before reaching extreme levels of fame, fortune, and success: Walt Disney, Henry Ford, Donald Trump, Dave Ramsey, H. J. Heinz, and Larry King.

Once people achieve success and fame, all of the attention goes to their current success, and we get a distorted view of what brought them there. We see them as brilliant when it may be they were just more persistent. Even the genius Albert Einstein said, "It's not that I'm so smart, it's just that I stay with problems longer."

Go for Quantity, then Refine
Persistence needs to be more than simple courage to try and try again—we must refine our approach.

For the subject of quantity vs. quality in the context of life decisions and progress, it's most accurate to say that **quantity is the path to quality**. When you can refine something over many attempts, improving it more with each iteration, you're bound to have greater success than if you meticulously planned out the perfect first try. This is interesting, because it means those obsessed with quality should aim for higher quantity to achieve their end goal.

This comparison of quality vs. quantity is the same as perfectionist thinking vs. imperfectionist thinking. Perfectionists aim for quality: they don't want to make a mistake; they want to get it right the first time; if they can't do it right, they won't do it. Imperfectionists aim for quantity: they'll accept a rough first try; they'll be happy to get it right the fifth time; if they can do it at all, even poorly, they will give it a shot.

Undoubtedly, when talking about *end results*, quality is preferred, but obsessing over quality can decrease it by interfering with (or skipping) the critical refinement process.

Veteran writers know that the way to write great content is to keep writing and refining. Writing is rarely finished in a first draft miracle. Ernest Hemingway said, "Writing is rewriting." Other examples:

- Exercise plans are refined as we see how our body reacts to different routines, weights, and workloads.
- Our social skills are refined through seeing reactions to different statements, jokes, questions, topics, and body language.
- Language is refined through many years and continues to evolve and become more versatile (LOLZ, u c how gr8 it is now?).

Life itself is a process. We're rarely "arriving" in that we can consider something complete; we're always in motion! For example, if a person wants to lose 50 pounds, what happens after that? Do they gain it back? Hopefully not, because that would defeat the purpose. The real goal is to reach and maintain a certain standard, and that is not done by planning for 30 days of perfect behavior; it's done by sustaining imperfect but purposeful behavior over the long term (such as the mini habit of doing 1+ push-up a day).

Focusing on quantity (not quality) of repetitions over time leads to consistency, which leads to habit formation, which is the heart of personal growth. When you engage in this process and a behavior becomes habitual, your subconscious will prefer it instead of resist it. That's victory. Can you see now why I cringe when I see so many people try to "get motivated" to achieve their goals? We need long-lasting habits to win, not short-lived motivational bursts.

Most advice out there tells you to dream big, but dreaming big does not mean you have to aim big. I'm one of the biggest dreamers I know—one dream of mine is to revolutionize the entertainment industry—and I focus exclusively on mini-sized goals. It was only when I let go of my perfect, big goals that my dreams started coming true in the areas of fitness, writing, and reading. Don't confuse dreaming big with making your dream into an overwhelming goal. **Your best chance to reach your big dreams is through small goals in quantity.**

Chapter 10

Application Guide

"I always find beauty in things that are odd and imperfect—they are much more interesting."

~ Marc Jacobs

© 2015 Stephen Guise

The Beginning of the End

Thank you for coming on this journey with me. Though this is a non-fiction book, I try to make my books enjoyable experiences as well as deliver helpful advice. That's why I add in things like the illustrations to begin each chapter.

When you finish this book, I want you to feel immeasurably empowered and believe that you can become an imperfectionist. Before we get into the solutions, I want to say something about the paths we take.

Kill the Notion of the Golden Path

Life is not a one-way, single-lane road. It's a sprawling, free-for-all field. If your goal is to get from point A to point B, the straight and obvious way does not have to be your path, and it may not be the best choice. The assumption of the perfectionist is that there is a golden path and that no other way will suffice.

I consider myself a resilient person today, and it's because I had an unexpected and shattering mental breakdown in 2011–2012. At my worst, I remember sitting in the corner of my bed, visibly shaking for no reason. It was not what I had in mind, and it was miserable, but in hindsight, it made me a stronger person. It effectively killed my notion of the golden path.

When you go through something awful and come out stronger, you realize that the best path is not so simple to define. Masochists aside, nobody enjoys going through painful experiences, but we learn and grow the most from them.

I'm not saying we should carelessly run into what hurts us most. I'm saying that even the worst detours have value. That is to say that *all paths* have some value, and while some are measurably better than others, finding the best one isn't as important as moving forward in life. Unequivocally, the worst choice is inaction. Perfectionists often choose inaction because, with an infinite number of possible paths, finding the perfect one is difficult to figure out. When pursuing some end, you can know where you want to go, but give yourself flexibility in your path to get there. If you keep your path flexible and practice perseverance, you're going to get many of the things you want in life.

Earlier, I mentioned my imperfect journey to becoming a writer. If I only accepted the straightforward way, I don't know what I'd be doing, but it wouldn't be this.

Every choice we make from this day on will be imperfect, so let's take comfort in that by allowing ourselves to choose without unnecessary guilt and self-criticism.

Solutions Summarized

Many of the solutions in this book involve a shift in mindset. But that's not immediately applicable. After all, how do you change the way you perceive the world? Like any change, it requires some amount of actionable practice.

To convert any of these mental shifts into an action, all you need to do is spend about a minute (or even less) to reflect on it each day. For example, the first general perfectionism solution is to change what you care about, so if you wanted to change in that way, you'd take a moment to remind yourself of this. This is an extremely powerful technique because it makes mental changes—which are critical, but challenging to adopt in their current form—into something clear and actionable.

Over time, you'll become more cognizant of the new way of thinking, and eventually, you'll adopt it as your *default* way of thinking. As you reflect on a perspective shift each day, you'll be far more likely to *act* according to it and get excellent results, which further embeds the idea into your psyche.

For these mental suggestions, I suggest a one-minute daily mini habit (as early in the day as possible, since they're mindset-related). Given the speed of thought, one minute is a significant amount of time to think on something, but it's simple and fast enough to fit it into each day without fail. This makes it a high-impact, low-effort, and low-sacrifice activity.

Before we get to the solutions, let me say you don't have to avoid perfectionism perfectly! This should go without saying, as imperfectionism is the goal, but it's important not to judge and beat yourself up if you catch yourself ruminating about a past event or acting like a perfectionist. Part of imperfectionism is being kind to and patient with yourself. And on that note …

Never use guilt as motivation.

I recently ruminated about an issue even after writing the rumination chapter. Recently, I saw an attractive woman at the gym. I walked up to her, asked her name, introduced myself, chatted a bit, and then asked for her number. She then told me she has a boyfriend. And after she said she'd see me around the gym, I uttered the regretful phrase, "Have fun with your boyfriend!"

Now, I meant well with that comment, but I can't imagine it came across well. It could be taken as a bitter, sarcastic comment from a rejected man. It could be taken as an inappropriate and strange sexual remark. There are simply no redeeming qualities about it, okay?

Naturally, I began to ruminate on this unfortunate choice of words. The reason I did so is why we ruminate at all—I cared. I care about romance and relationships, and it'd be my preference not to say horrendous things to women I fancy. But I recognized it, knew how to terminate it, and successfully moved forward. In other words: **individual occurrences of perfectionism (and its subsets) don't matter—your response to them matters.**

General Perfectionism (2 Solutions)

1. Change what you care about action: For one minute each day, reflect on and imagine caring about what the list below describes.

- Don't care about results. Care about putting in the work.
- Don't care about problems. Care about making progress despite them. Or if you must fix something, focus on the solution.
- Don't care what other people think. Care about who you want to be and what you want to do.
- Care less about doing it right. Care more about doing it at all.
- Don't care about failure. Care about success.
- Don't care about timing. Care about the task.

2. Imperfectionist process action: For one minute each day, consider the imperfectionist process in terms of your plans that day. Imagine how one or more key goals you have for the day can benefit from accepting imperfection in each stage of the process.

1. Imperfect thoughts and ideas.
2. Imperfect decision.
3. Imperfect action.
4. Imperfect adaptation.
5. Imperfect, but successful result.

Here's an example of how that thought process might go for working out:

1. I'd like to work out at the gym today, but I'm not sure my routine idea is ideal and I'm somewhat self-conscious of my body at the gym.
2. I'm going to exercise, even though I will miss out on some other things.
3. Now that I'm exercising, I don't seem to have a lot of energy, but I'm still doing it.
4. Ouch! I dropped the dumbbell on my toe. I won't do that next time.
5. In spite of my doubts, imperfections, and swollen toe, I just exercised to get stronger and healthier!

The fifth step of the imperfectionist process is crucial, because it makes the preceding imperfection all but irrelevant. After you've exercised, after you've pulled weeds in the garden, or after you've written a few pages of your novel, you've done something to be proud of, and it doesn't matter if the process wasn't impressive!

Unrealistic Expectations (4 Solutions)

1. Adjust your expectations action: For one minute, check your expectations.

Choose to have high general expectations and low to no specific expectations. This means that, in general, you take on an optimistic outlook regarding yourself and your life. You're confident in your abilities. But you realize that in any specific instance, on a macro and micro level, an outcome can be poor. For example, in a conversation, you might say one thing you regret, or regret the entire conversation—these both fall under a "specific" instance. Because of this, you don't have specific expectations for any individual event or undertaking. You take any individual failures in stride, knowing that they're a small part of a much bigger picture.

What are your expectations for events on your schedule? If they're high, adjust them lower, or, better yet, try to drop expectations and go in with a "We'll see what happens" perspective. This won't negatively impact your enjoyment of positive events; it will only enhance it while protecting you from negative surprises. Try to be optimistic in general, but don't tie your hopes to any situation—this helps you be flexible when confronting imperfections.

2. Decide what's "enough" action: This idea can be applied specifically or in general. In a specific perfectionism problem area, decide what will be enough for you today. Alternatively, you can generally decide that your life as it is now is enough (contentment). The best way to make this a mini habit is to spend a minute per day practicing contentment with what you have.

Take responsibility for what is "enough." Only you can decide what is enough for you; don't let society's message of "never enough" become your motto. In a case-by-case basis, you can decide that something is not enough. You might be surprised at just how little you need in some areas. My apartment is only 150 square feet, and that's enough for me. It's just like this previously mentioned quote:

"People call me a perfectionist, but I'm not. I'm a rightist. I do something until it's right, and then I move on to the next thing."
~ James Cameron

Notice how he takes control of what is enough. It's a personal decision. The problem of perfectionism is not the aspect of striving for excellence, but striving for impossible standards that you didn't personally set. If you're aiming for impossible, it's because you think someone is watching over your shoulder.

3. Lower the bar action: Create between one and four mini habits of your choice. Visit http://minihabits.com/mini-habit-ideas/ for ideas.

The easiest way to lower the bar is with mini habits, which train you to understand that no action is too small or imperfect to be insignificant. This works on your expectations on a deeper level because it eventually rewires your subconscious to accept smaller bits of progress and success. The issue with unrealistic expectations is typically that they freeze you, as you don't want to jump in unless you are assured of supreme victory on the first try. Mini habits break through this barrier.

If you already have mini habits or want to create one for this specifically, come up with one idea to lower the bar for action in an important area of your choice each day depending on your circumstances (examples: decide to be willing to write content with your cell phone, exercise at night, run in the rain, exercise while tired, etc.). This one is hard to make into a daily habit, because lowering the bar is situational, which is why I suggest generating ideas that you might execute later.

4. Focus on the process action: Look at your day ahead, pick your most daunting challenge, and break it down into a process you can follow. When the time comes, you'll be reminded of the process and your challenging task will become much less stressful and will seem more doable!

Focus on the process and stop caring about results. This is another objective accomplished with mini habits (which are an anti-perfectionist Swiss Army knife). When someone has unrealistic expectations, it means they desire a particular result that's either impossible to achieve or very unlikely without considerable grit and practice. The amazing thing is that focusing on the process guarantees better results, while focusing on results distracts you from the process needed to obtain them. Results are always the conclusion of whatever process precedes them. Give yourself some mini habits in the areas where you want results, and they'll redirect your focus to the process.

Rumination (5 Solutions)

1. Accepting the past action: For one minute, reflect on the permanent, unchangeable nature of the past.

You can accept the past as permanently unchangeable by creating a daily reminder that you can't change what's happened. This needs to be processed logically first before it can be processed emotionally. Denial of reality fuels the emotions that enable rumination.

2. Replacing rumination action: Take action directly against your rumination (preferably with a related mini habit). If you're ruminating about losing a client for your business, set out to get one new client or make one call related to that end. If you're ruminating about an argument, make amends with that person or plan a really fun day with a different friend. If you're upset about an unfixable tragedy, do your mini habits or find another way to continue moving your life forward.

One of the best ways to change your mind about something is to act according to the change you wish to make. If you're ruminating about the past, acting in the present (especially in the area of rumination) is the best way to stop it. For example, if you're ruminating about a poor job interview, applying for more jobs is the best thing you can do. If you're ruminating about a relationship, going out and meeting new people is the best thing you can do to move on. If the rumination is in regards to a tragic event, a general decision to live life to the fullest is ideal. Mini habits help tremendously with this as well, because their low bar to action is low enough for emotionally drained people to still engage with.

Glenda Lynn, a reader of *Mini Habits*, sent me this email:

"This Wednesday night my granddaughter was killed in a car accident. She had her 18-month-old son with her, and luckily, he escaped unharmed, but of course, it was a huge tragedy for our family. But, thanks to the mini habits and the HappyRitual app, I have managed to continue with the routines and better habits I started previous to this horrid event. I thought you'd like to know that it has actually been a godsend to help me to keep going in as healthy a manner as possible. It might be something you could add to your classes. Is there any research showing how routines help us to get through catastrophic events?"

Habits are an effective way to avoid being crippled by catastrophes. We all need to develop good habits and simple objectives that bring us easy, small victories in the face of feeling defeated. This can help us survive the worst life has to throw at us.

3. Understanding chance and failure action: If you're ruminating about a negative outcome or mistake, take one minute to determine if it was because of a chance result or failure. If it is pure failure, think of a different strategy to try. If it is pure chance, try the same strategy again as soon as you can. If it is a combination of the two, continue to try while tweaking your strategy accordingly.

Failure is when you alone are responsible for the outcome—such as if you trip, add the wrong potion to the concoction, or misspell "mispell." Chance is when someone else is involved, especially when they are making the decision —like inviting someone to dinner, asking for a raise, competing on *American Idol*, or getting a lower-than-desired grade on your essay.

An interesting example is pursuing personal goals like exercise—that's more of a failure if you don't reach them, because it's completely up to you if you go to the gym or not. That's why people succeed when they try mini habits—

it's a fundamentally different strategy to reach your goals than conventional "wisdom."

The common idea that beats rumination is to keep trying. Understanding chance and failure aren't just useful for strategy; they're also useful for emotionally adjusting and logically reacting to negative results. When you realize your "failure" was actually just a chance result, it's much easier to give yourself a break and put yourself back out there!

4. Change your self-talk action: If ruminating on a topic, remove "should have" from your mind and substitute "could have" in the sense of another possible option. If not ruminating, think of the current difficulties in your life and choose to see them as challenges instead of "hard" or "difficult" situations.

"Should have" is guilt about the past. "Could have" is opportunity for the future. Your self-talk has a lot to do with your perspective. And as one of the easiest things to change, it can have a dramatic impact on your life fairly quickly.

Bonus tip: Life problems? They're not "hard" or "difficult" or even "problems"—they're challenges! That's an empowering perspective that makes you want to rise to the challenge in the same fun yet intense way you would respond to a challenge to compete in ping pong.

5. Timer hacks action: At least once per day, use one of these timer tools to spark yourself to action on a task that will directly improve or take your mind off of your rumination area(s).

Be active. No matter the topic of rumination, the answer is activity. The more active you are in the present moment, the less opportunity you have to ruminate and the more opportunities you have to create a life right now worth thinking about (instead of your object of rumination). The best action strategy in general is having daily mini habits. For doing additional work, I recommend timer-based techniques such as the ones mentioned in chapter 6 (Rumination):

- The Countdown Starter: When the timer runs out, you must start your task immediately.
- The Decision Countdown: You must make a firm decision before the timer runs out!
- The Focus Timer: For X minutes, you must focus on one task of choice (with strict rules for distractions).

- The Pomodoro Technique: Work 25 minutes, rest 5 minutes. Repeat.
- The Work & Play Carousel: Work for an hour, relax for an hour. Repeat.

Need for Approval (4 Solutions)

Needing approval means that you struggle to be yourself and lack confidence in yourself (especially in social situations). You can improve your confidence with this four-pronged approach:

1. Chemical confidence boost action: For two minutes before any situation requiring confidence, stand in a "power pose." In a wide stance, put your arms straight out or put your hands on your hips. Or while seated, put your hands behind your head with your elbows out.

Chemically boost confidence by assuming power poses for two minutes or so (it sounds crazy, but it's proven!) before any occasion when you want to be confident (interviews, social events, dates, meetings, speeches, presentations, etc.). Work to make your general body language more confident so that this can become a long-term change.

2. Faking confidence action: To make this specific and actionable, commit to act confidently (even if you feel otherwise) in at least one situation per day.

"Fake" confidence by acting confidently even when you don't feel it. Sometimes you have to fake it before you'll feel it and be confident for real. Faking confidence is not the same as being a fake person; it's more like practicing something you're not yet skilled at.

Pretend you're very confident in any situation. You can exaggerate the effect, and you might be surprised how naturally it comes across to others. If you go to a store every day, you can practice being completely confident with the cashier. Don't worry if you feel nervous while doing it—that goes away in time.

3. Change your benchmark action: For any task that intimidates you or that you feel you don't measure up to, lower your benchmark to something you *know* you can do.

The easiest and most immediate way to become more confident is to change what you're trying to be confident about. Instead of trying to be James Bond, try to be a person who can say "Hi" to people, and your confidence in meeting your benchmark will rise. The only reason people aren't confident is because of a preconceived standard about how well they should measure up in an area. When you drop that preconceived notion and customize your confidence, you'll be yourself and naturally exude confidence.

Don't compare your running skills to your marathon-running friend or a cheetah; set your benchmark at tortoise level if you must. For social interactions, don't use the movies as your benchmark. Real life interaction is not scripted and more awkward.

4. Rebellion action: Perform an act of rebellion against social norms or expectations once per day.

The opposite of needing approval is rebellion, and so those who have a problem with need for approval need to practice rebelling. There are a great number of ways a person can rebel against approval in a safe, legal way. The easiest way to practice is to act unusually in public. This is something people are typically embarrassed to do, but singing a song out loud in a grocery store every once in a while doesn't hurt anyone. Most likely, people will laugh.

If you need approval from a certain person and you feel the need to change, think of a small but symbolic way you could rebel against their control over you. There's no need to go over the top to prove a point (though if you need approval, you're unlikely to overdo it). The idea is to practice living in your own way until you get used to not needing others to tell you how to live. Small symbolic gestures like singing out loud, lying down on the floor in public, or even talking to strangers are great ways to show the world, and yourself, that you're in charge of your life.

Concern over Mistakes (4 Solutions)

1. Accomplishment journal action: Decide where to write your accomplishment journal (notepad, computer, cell phone) and write at least one thing you've accomplished (or a positive trait you have) once per day until you can't think of any more.

This is not a big time commitment—it's taking a few minutes to write down some of the good things you've done and become. People who struggle with Impostor Syndrome are poor at internalizing their accomplishments. Writing them down can help tremendously and make them more tangible in your mind.

2. Binary mindset action: In an area that you fear making mistakes, create a binary perspective. Then go out and get the win! To make this a daily action, require yourself to define a binary setup applicable to your life OR to achieve a binary win that you've defined. You could create ideas for the first few days, and then switch to application.

If you're concerned over mistakes, you're going to be concerned your entire life, because mistakes are frequent happenings for everyone. The binary mindset is an effortless way to take your mind off mistakes you might make and onto the actions you have the opportunity to take. Instead of seeing a situation as going from 1 (poorly) to 10 (perfectly), see situations as 0 (not doing anything) and 1 (doing something). When you focus on doing things and counting that as an automatic success, you'll make more progress in life and do so in a more relaxed manner.

Examples:

- Say "Hi" to a person you find attractive = win.
- Send any email to a person of interest (for business, networking, or a specific request) = win.
- Write a story outline (it doesn't have to be good!) = win.
- Publish a book = win.
- Give a speech = win.

A person might say "Hi" to someone and be ignored, send an email proposal that is rejected, write a story about a penguin going to prison, publish a book that doesn't sell, and stutter along to boos from the crowd. These are still five wins. The resilience built, the courage generated, the empowerment you'll feel by putting yourself out there and the valuable feedback you'll receive will make this one of the most productive days in your life. And that's the worst-case scenario—negative results in all of these cases are unlikely. Failure is never as discouraging as doing nothing is. That's why the binary mindset is gold.

3. Easier success action: Create and pursue daily mini habits to make daily success too easy to turn down. Make success easier than failure, and you'll succeed.

4. Modular success action: When your day begins, don't aim for success, aim for progress, and accept it in *any* size. Think about this idea for one minute per day.

Don't see success as being a clean, perfect milestone like losing 100 pounds. Mentally smash your big goals with a sledgehammer. When they shatter into hundreds of pieces, pick up the smallest piece and consider that the previously big goal wouldn't be complete without it. See success as modular and let progress be your new definition of success. When you see progress as success, you'll place less emphasis on reaching a mistake-free milestone and more on what you can do next to move forward.

After seeking progress for some time, you'll end up with the larger accomplishments you wanted all along.

Doubts about Actions (3 Solutions)

1. Anti-projection action: When you're doubtful of doing something and projecting negative scenarios, write them down in detail. Have a predetermined place to write it down or you won't do it. Then experiment in that situation and compare the actual results to your projection. Before you start jumping off cliffs (an action that merits doubting), you can start with safer things like talking to strangers, going to the gym when you're tired, or asking for favors.

Be wary of projecting and rely as much as possible on experiments and experience to base conclusions on. We tend to doubt things that are new, which are naturally unknown. Until you try something, you can't know how it will go. Projections are often inaccurate, especially when it comes to anything requiring effort. When we subconsciously want to avoid something such as an activity that requires effort, our projections will be inaccurate and negatively biased.

2. Faster decisions action: Once per day, present yourself with four options relevant to your plans—such as what to eat for lunch or dinner, chores/tasks you could do right now, people you could call on the phone, etc. —and write them down quickly on a piece of paper. Take your time to formulate the ideas, but once they are all written down, circle one of them *as fast as you can*, feeling at least reasonably comfortable with your choice.

Scratch out the others emphatically. Aim for less than 10 seconds to choose. Whichever one you circle, commit to doing it that day. The more you do this, the more you'll see and experience that making fast decisions on relatively trivial matters (and sometimes even important ones) is one of the greatest skills a person can have.

In making decisions, we deliberate (weigh our options) and then implement (take action). Procrastinators tend to revisit deliberation even after they've found the best step to take. If you practice terminating the deliberation phase and moving quickly to implementation, you'll see there's a limit to the usefulness of deliberation. Make faster decisions.

3. Outcome analysis action: For an action you're doubting, run it through this easy analysis:

Worst case severity: Think of the worst thing that could happen and rate the severity 1-10. If you're considering starting a garden, you don't have to think of things like, "being struck by lightning in the garden as I'm stepping on a wasp." Choose a realistic worst-case scenario.

Worst case likelihood: Rate the likelihood of your worst-case scenario happening (very unlikely, unlikely, 50/50, likely, very likely).

Best case benefit: Think of the best-case scenario and rate its impact. Don't think of things like, "While harvesting green beans, a beautiful woman in a white dress approaches me." What's the realistic best-case scenario and how great would it be?

Best case likelihood: Rate the likelihood of your best-case scenario happening (very unlikely, unlikely, 50/50, likely, very likely).

Most likely case: Think about what's most likely to happen and how you'd feel about it.

Estimate the outcome probability and impact of potential actions. For example, starting a business has a high chance of failure statistically, but the impact of failure may be bearable, and while the chance of success may be slim, the impact could be life-changing. Don't keep this information vague, or you'll struggle to leave the deliberation phase.

This is simple, and when you write it down, you'll have a much easier time analyzing your decision to see if your doubts have merit or not. Interpreting the results is important, too. It's a function of consequences and their likelihood.

Example 1: Your worst-case scenario for skateboarding might be a broken arm that you'd rate 9/10 severity. Your best-case scenario might be a 6/10 in fun, but if the odds of a broken arm are extremely unlikely and the best-case scenario is very likely, it's probably a favorable risk to take, despite the severity of the worst-case scenario. Just be careful out there.

Example 2: In playing the lottery, the worst case is losing a dollar or two (1/10 severity) and the best case is winning a lot of money (10/10 benefit). If you only look at risk and reward—as many do—it seems like playing the lottery is a great idea. But the worst case (not winning) is *almost guaranteed to happen*, which makes it an unfavorable risk, despite the favorable risk/reward consequences.

Application Advice

This book contains many solutions for perfectionism. One frustration I have with self-help books is that they'll give you numerous solutions with no framework for choosing and integrating them into your life. To me, this is one of the most important parts of solving problems in life. You have to have some kind of structured plan to accept and implement new strategies and goals.

The first question is: how many goals are you going to pursue at once?

This is not an easy question to answer, especially because the size of each goal differs. It's not the same thing to aim to drink a glass of water compared to practicing piano for an hour a day. Plus, we all have dozens of things we'd like to be doing in any given moment. The standard technique to handle this is to try to prioritize what matters and then estimate how much you can handle at once. But we tend to overestimate what we can accomplish consistently, which is why people quit their goals so often.

In *Mini Habits*, I recommended no more than four mini habits at a time, and these solutions are in mini habit form (because mini habits are naturally an "imperfectionist" way of viewing a goal and are ideal to reliably change our behavior). Based on the many responses I've received, I'm going to stick with that recommendation. Yes, some people have reported success with five or six mini habits at a time, but they are the exception and their chance of failure is higher. For most people, two or three mini habits at a time is ideal.

You know what a perfectionist would try? They'd try to fix everything right now, all at the same time. They'd fail, too. A key part of imperfectionism is *patience*. You may not change your life overnight, but you will enjoy the process of changing into an imperfectionist!

If you've read *Mini Habits* and you have some mini habits in place, don't be so eager to add more to your plate. Being overwhelmed does not help productivity; simplicity does! But these solutions are slightly different than trying to form a good habit. Given the nature of these solutions, a new mini habit strategy is needed, and that strategy is project-based mini habits.

Project-based Mini Habits

I was originally planning on including this strategy in the next *Mini Habits* book I write. Typically, mini habits are pursued in order to form habits in key areas. But what if a person already has key habits in place and simply wants to work on other areas like perfectionism as a project or experiment? In that case, you can use a project-based mini habit plan.

Mini habit plans are long-term pursuits of the same set of behaviors, but project-based mini habits are flexible and interchangeable. The difference is that for a project-based mini habit, you are more focused on developing sets of related skills that work together instead of developing single habits to improve your life. Given the 22 perfectionism solutions presented in this book, a project-based mini habit plan makes the most sense in application because:

1. By experimenting, you could find certain techniques to be more effective than others at changing your perfectionism. If you only chose three solutions for the long term, you could miss out on more effective ones.
2. Perfectionism is best conquered with a multifaceted attack. This is because we're attempting to change a general mindset. Perfectionism has a lot of roots, and can be weakened by systematically attacking them.

One day you might struggle with concern over mistakes and so need to practice using a binary mindset. Another day you might struggle with need for approval and so need to practice rebelling against it. The idea isn't necessarily to switch between these every day, but to have practiced them both to have firsthand experience of how to apply both skills as needed.

It's a similar strategy to Ben Franklin's "13 virtues." Franklin was a driven man who, funnily enough, attempted to become perfect. His idea was to take 13 virtuous traits and attempt to master them one at a time, one week at a time. Each week, he'd allow himself to slip up in other areas, but focused all of his energy on succeeding in the chosen area, be it sincerity, justice, or moderation. When he mastered one area, he'd fail at the other, but he said he had improved quite a bit overall in the process. While his goal was becoming perfect in these areas, he went about the task in an imperfectionist way, because he didn't try to do them all at once.

It's fitting for us that we fall short of the goal to be "perfectly imperfectionist" in our way of thinking. Franklin's strategy, combined with the power of mini habits to enable action, will lead us closer to the goal of ultimate internal freedom. Here's what you can do.

I like to use a giant calendar to track my mini habits. And the way I do it is draw a check mark on each day that I complete them. Since I've been doing mini habits for a couple years and have conquered the initial resistance that used to prevent me from doing what I want to do, it has become more of a choice of how I want to spend my time (rather than struggling to get myself to spend it wisely). Now, I can write fiction, non-fiction, a book or blog post, a guest post, and more. I can read, or meditate, or both. Or I could choose to focus wholly on one project.

Using project-based mini habits with a physical calendar is easiest. You simply write the mini habits you want to pursue on the day that you start them. For example:

May 22: Write 50 words toward book, read two pages per day.

On that day, and every day afterwards (until a change occurs), a check means that you completed those mini habits. But say you just read this book, you're comfortable with your reading and writing habits, and you want to practice imperfectionism for the next month instead. On June 1, you could write:

1. Practice one act of rebellion.
2. Reflect on list of imperfectionist cares for one minute.
3. Apply binary mindset to one objective.

These three actions would become your new mini habits until changed. From that date onward, your check marks would mean that you've completed those three mini habits (and not the reading and writing ones from May 22). This is a simple visual way to swap mini habits in and out as you see fit. It greatly decreases the chance for habit formation, but it can develop your skills in a broad category like practicing the numerous ways to become more of an imperfectionist.

This may also be appealing for people who aren't sure they have that go-to behavior they want to habitualize, but instead want to explore and experiment with a number of different behaviors. And finally, this method is perfect for those who take a project-based approach to life (with entrepreneurs, this is common). After you publish your book using your 50 words a day mini habit, you can switch to researching one idea or study per day for the next project.

This works best with a calendar—physical or digital—that allows you to write on it and check off days. A habit-tracking app would make switching mini habits in and out more difficult, which makes sense because habit-tracking apps are for forming habits, and this strategy isn't to form habits as much as it is to experiment, complete projects, and cycle related sets of mini habits to conquer a multi-root problem like perfectionism. As for how often you switch your mini habits, that's up to you.

If you're a general perfectionist, I recommend spending one week at a time on each of the five subsets and one week on general imperfectionism, making the complete cycle six weeks long. This will give you a good feel of how the solutions work for you. You can adjust if you think you struggle with one subset more than the others. For example, maybe you'll want to spend two weeks on rumination solutions.

Visit http://imperfectionistbook.com for more plan ideas.

The End of the End

The first section of this chapter was titled, "The Beginning of the End." Now we've reached the end of the end, but the end of this book may signify the beginning of an exciting change for you. As the examples throughout the book describe, I've personally experienced the power of these changes in my life. I'm confident you can do the same.

Imperfectionists aren't so ironic as to have perfect lives: they're just happier, healthier, and more productive at doing what matters. Perfectionism is limitation and imperfectionism is freedom, so give the solutions in this book a try and begin your transformation into an imperfectionist. You'll be glad you did.

I wish you the best on your imperfect journey forward!

Cheers,
Stephen Guise

There's More!

Mini Habits
If you haven't yet, I strongly recommend reading my first book, *Mini Habits*. While it's not imperative to read *Mini Habits* to benefit from this book, there is a definite synergy between them. If you read *Mini Habits*, you'll understand why these imperfectionist practices are in mini habit form.

Based on the science, *Mini Habits* is arguably the most effective habit formation strategy in the world; and based on reviews, it's arguably the most beloved. People can't help but talk about the strategy that's changed their life!

Mini Habits Book: http://amazon.com/dp/B00HGKNBDK

Mini Habit Mastery
If you prefer video and want to learn the mini habits concept, you can take the Mini Habit Mastery Video Course. It retails for $149, but you can use coupon code "**imperfectionist**" to get it for just $59 (that's $90 off!). The book and the course are leaders in ratings and satisfaction (the course is rated 5 stars from 40+ reviews), and I guarantee my products' reviews are genuine.

Mini Habit Mastery HD Video Course: http://udemy.com/mini-habit-mastery/

Deep Existence Tuesday Messages
Every Tuesday, I write about smart life strategies and email them to subscribers. People have told me this content is life-changing. When you sign up, you can look through the archives of previous messages of interest. These are exclusive to subscribers and free. The benefit for me is communication: I can tell you when my next book or course is available!

Tuesday email sign-up: http://deepexistence.com/subscribe/

Thank You and Contact

Thank you so much for reading *How to Be an Imperfectionist*. I hope you enjoyed it.

If you believe this book shares an important message, please leave a review on Amazon. Reviews (in quantity and in rating) are the main metric people use to judge a book's content. And if you become an imperfectionist, please come back and tell other readers (and me) about your progress!

Every single review has a huge impact on others' willingness to read a book, and if this strategy changes your life, you can change someone else's life by spreading the word. The impact and reach of this book is up to you. *Mini Habits* is proof of this. Because readers have reviewed and shared it, it will soon be read all over the world! Will you help me spread the message of *How to Be an Imperfectionist* across our perfectionistic world?

When you finish this book, please tell someone else about it or let them borrow your copy!

Bonus content: http://imperfectionistbook.com
Contact Stephen: sguise@deepexistence.com

References

[1] Merriam-Webster.com. 'Perfectionism' | N.p., 2015. Web. 9 May 2015.

[2] FMPS; Frost, Marten, Lahart, & Rosenblate (1990). Cognitive Therapy and Research, 14, 449–568.

[3] Stöber, Joachim. 'The Frost Multidimensional Perfectionism Scale Revisited: More Perfect With Four (Instead Of Six) Dimensions'. Personality and Individual Differences 24.4 (1998): 481-491.

[4] Hewitt, Paul L. et al. 'The Multidimensional Perfectionism Scale: Reliability, Validity, And Psychometric Properties In Psychiatric Samples.'. Psychological Assessment 3.3 (1991): 464-468.

[5] Hill, Robert W. et al. 'A New Measure Of Perfectionism: The Perfectionism Inventory'. Journal of Personality Assessment 82.1 (2004): 80-91.

[6] Oprah.com,. 'Why Brene Brown Says Perfectionism Is A 20-Ton Shield'. N.p., 2015. Web. 10 May 2015.

[7] Fry, P. S., and D. L. Debats. 'Perfectionism And The Five-Factor Personality Traits As Predictors Of Mortality In Older Adults'. Journal of Health Psychology 14.4 (2009): 513-524.

[8] Blatt, Sidney J. 'The Destructiveness Of Perfectionism: Implications For The Treatment Of Depression.'. American Psychologist 50.12 (1995): 1003-1020.

[9] Flett, Gordon L., Paul L. Hewitt, and Marnin J. Heisel. 'The Destructiveness Of Perfectionism Revisited: Implications For The Assessment Of Suicide Risk And The Prevention Of Suicide.'. Review of General Psychology 18.3 (2014): 156-172.

[10] Blatt, 'The Destructiveness Of Perfectionism' (1995)

[11] Hamachek, Don E. 'Psychodynamics of Normal and Neurotic Perfectionism'. Psychology: A Journal of Human Behavior (1978): n.p. Web. 10 May 2015.

[12] FMPS; Frost, Marten, Lahart, & Rosenblate (1990). Cognitive Therapy and Research, 14, 465.

[13] Greenspon, Thomas. '"Healthy Perfectionism" Is an Oxymoron!'. Davidsongifted.org. n.p., 2000. Web. 10 May 2015.

[14] Pacht, Asher R. 'Reflections On Perfection'. American Psychologist, 39.4 (1984): 386-390.

[15] Greenspon, "Healthy Perfectionism" (2000).

[16] Nielsen.com, 'Shifts in Viewing: The Cross-Platform Report Q2 2014'. N.p., 2014. Web. 8 May 2015.

[17] Biswas, Aviroop et al. (2015) 'Sedentary Time and its Association with Risk for Disease Incidence, Mortality, and Hospitalization in Adults'. Annals of Internal Medicine, 162.2: 123. Web.

[18] Morrow, Jon. 'Make Money Blogging: 20 Lessons Going to $100K per Month'. Boost Blog Traffic. N.p., 2014. Web. 8 May 2015.

[19] Nytimes.com,. 'To Err Is Human, And Maybe Also Psychologically Healthy'. N.p., 2011. Web. 10 May 2015.

[20] New England Patriots,. 'Game Notes: Patriots Have Won 72 Straight Home Games When Leading At Half'. N.p., 2014. Web. 10 May 2015.

[21] Neal, David T., Wendy Wood, and Jeffrey M. Quinn. 'Habits—A Repeat Performance'. Current Directions in Psychological Science 15.4 (2006): 198-202.

[22] Snopes.com,. 'Carried Away'. N.p., 2015. Web. 11 May 2015.

[23] Cuddy, Amy. 'Your Body Language Shapes Who You Are'. Ted.com. N.p., 2012. Web. 11 May 2015.

[24] Cuddy 'Your Body Language Shapes Who You Are' (2012)

[25] Wendy Wood et al., 'Habits—A Repeat Performance' (2006)

[26] Corson-Knowles, Tom. 'List Of The Top #100 Most Competitive Amazon Kindle Bestseller Categories'. TCK Publishing. N.p., 2014. Web. 11 May 2015.

[27] Graber, Cynthia. 'Snake Oil Salesmen Were On To Something'. Scientificamerican.com. N.p., 2007. Web. 11 May 2015.

[28] Swanson, D., R. Block, and S. A. Mousa. 'Omega-3 Fatty Acids EPA And DHA: Health Benefits Throughout Life'. Advances in Nutrition: An International Review Journal 3.1 (2012): 1-7.

[29] NPR.org,. 'A History Of 'Snake Oil Salesmen''. N.p., 2013. Web. 11 May 2015.

[30] Oxforddictionaries.com,. 'Lever: Definition Of Lever In Oxford Dictionary (American English) (US)'. N.p., 2015. Web. 11 May 2015.

[31] McGonigal Ph.D., Kelly (2011-12-29). The Willpower Instinct: How Self-Control Works, Why It Matters, and What You Can Do to Get More of It (p. 215). Penguin Publishing Group. Kindle Edition.

[32] Forgas, J. P., Kipling D., Williams, & Laham, S. M. (2005). Social Motivation: Conscious and Unconscious Processes. Cambridge, UK: Cambridge UP, 64. Print.

[33] Luttrell, Marcus (2007-06-12). Lone Survivor: The Eyewitness Account of Operation Redwing and the Lost Heroes of SEAL Team 10 (p. 135). Little, Brown and Company. Kindle Edition.

[34] Pychyl, Timothy. 'The Pernicious Perils Of Perfectionism'. Psychology Today. N.p., 2010. Web. 11 May 2015.

[35] Kahneman, D. (2011-10-25). Thinking, Fast and Slow (p. 112). Farrar, Straus and Giroux. Kindle Edition.

[36] The Pomodoro Technique®,. 'GET STARTED -'. N.p., 2015. Web. 12

May 2015.

[37] Stats.oecd.org,. 'Average Annual Hours Actually Worked Per Worker'. N.p., 2015. Web. 11 May 2015.

[38] Epley, Nicholas, and Juliana Schroeder. 'Mistakenly Seeking Solitude.'. Journal of Experimental Psychology: General 143.5 (2014): 1980-1999.

[39] Frost, R. O., Trepanier, K. L., Brown, E. J., Heimburg, R. G., Juster, H. R., Leung, A. W., and Makris, G. S. (1997), "Self-Monitoring of Mistakes among Subjects High and Low in Concern over Mistakes," Cognitive Therapy and Research, 21, 209–222.

[40] Brown, E. J. et al. "Relationship of Perfectionism to…"

[41] Goldman, Matt, and Justin Rao. 'Effort Vs. Concentration: The Asymmetric Impact Of Pressure On NBA Performance'. N.p., 2012. Web. 8 Feb. 2015.

[42] Hewitt, Paul L., Gordon L. Flett, and Evelyn Ediger. 'Perfectionism Traits And Perfectionistic Self-Presentation In Eating Disorder Attitudes, Characteristics, And Symptoms'. International Journal of Eating Disorders 18.4 (1995): 319.

[43] Thompson, T., Foreman, P., and Martin, F. (2000), "Impostor Fears and Perfectionistic Concern over Mistakes," Personality and Individual Differences, 29(4) (October), 629–647. doi:10.1016/s0191-8869(99)00218-4.

[44] Goldsmith, Donald, and Marcia Bartusiak. E=Einstein. New York: Sterling Pub. Co., 2006: p. 258. Print.

[45] Thompson et al. "Impostor Fears."

[46] Sakulku, Jaruwan, and James Alexander. 'The Impostor Phenomenon'. International Journal of Behavioral Science 6.1 (2011): 84. Web. 8 Nov. 2014.

[47] Sakulku et al. "The Impostor Phenomenon."

[48] Frijda, Nico H. 'The Laws Of Emotion.'. American Psychologist 43.5 (1988): 349-358.

CPSIA information can be obtained at www.ICGtesting.com
Printed in the USA
LVOW06s1823080915

453275LV00002B/511/P